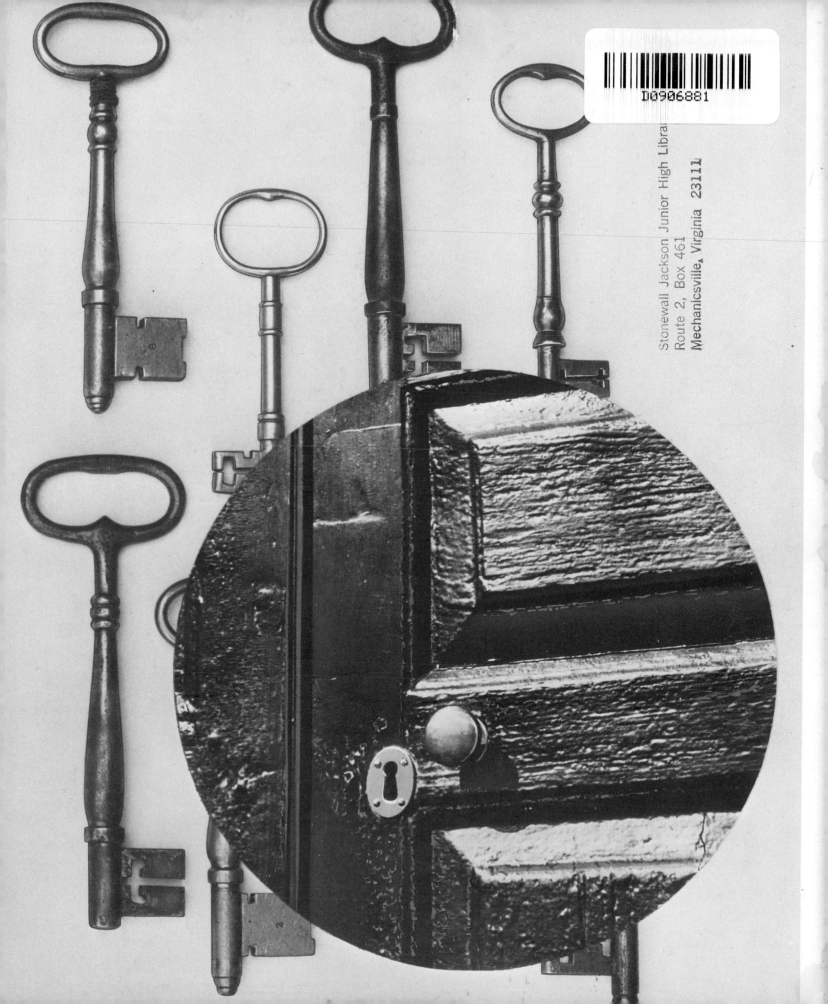

COLONIAL WILLIAMSBURG

Its Buildings and Gardens

COLONIAL WILLIAMSBURG

Its Buildings and Gardens

A DESCRIPTIVE TOUR OF THE RESTORED CAPITAL

OF THE BRITISH COLONY OF VIRGINIA

Second Revised Edition

BY

A. LAWRENCE KOCHER

AND

HOWARD DEARSTYNE

The COLONIAL WILLIAMSBURG FOUNDATION
Williamsburg, Virginia

Distributed by
HOLT, RINEHART AND WINSTON
New York, New York

Distributed simultaneously in Canada by Holt, Rinehart and
Winston of Canada, Limited.

Previous editions copyright 1949, 1961.

Library of Congress Cataloging in Publication Data

Kocher, Alfred Lawrence.
  Colonial Williamsburg, its buildings and gardens.

  Bibliography: p. 99
  Includes index.
  1. Historic buildings—Virginia—Williamsburg.
2. Williamsburg, Va.—Buildings. I. Dearstyne,
Howard, joint author. II. Title.
F234.W7K6 1976   917.55′4252′044   75–40353
ISBN 0–87935–035–0 (Colonial Williamsburg)
        0–03–089913–3 (Holt, Rinehart and Winston)

Printed in the United States of America

FOREWORD

THE VALUE of history lies in the perspective it gives us as we take up the problems of the present. Lawrence Kocher and Howard Dearstyne, by making us see here the intimate daily family life of eighteenth-century Williamsburg and the society of which it was a part, help us even more to see ourselves and our own time in sharper focus.

And insight, above everything else, is the purpose of Colonial Williamsburg—one-time capital of the great and powerful Virginia colony and the only capital of our colonial period which, after more than a century of sleep, could be awakened and reconstructed in its original form.

We hope that millions of Americans will find time and opportunity to visit Colonial Williamsburg in order that they may have the experience of stepping out of the present and losing themselves temporarily in the significant past. There is no better way for the modern American, man, woman, or child, to get a real emotional sense of the depth of his roots and the meaning of our nation's past.

Those who read this book—like those who come to Colonial Williamsburg—are urged to consider it only a foundation. The building of a free world can never be finished. We in our time must make our contribution. Colonial Williamsburg lives today to help all of us to feel strongly our heritage of liberty in order that we may build a better America and a better world in the twentieth century.

Colonial Williamsburg reminds us that the foundation of modern America is spiritual—a faith which began to take shape in Williamsburg and to be expressed there by some of the greatest of our forefathers. Nowhere else in colonial America was the democratic faith on which our nation has been built more eloquently expressed.

I think we cannot drink too deeply at this spring of our history. I think the authors in this book have helped you and me immeasurably to see the past so that we may understand and deal more effectively with the present.

KENNETH CHORLEY

President, Colonial Williamsburg
1935–1958

FOREWORD TO THE SECOND REVISED EDITION

OVER THE quarter-century since its first appearance, this publication has been filling a demand met by no other volume in the expanding list of Colonial Williamsburg books. At once authoritative and handsome, it has been several times reprinted and is now revised a second time to keep its text and pictures up to date with the progress of the past in Williamsburg.

The senior author, Lawrence Kocher, retired from Colonial Williamsburg in 1954, continuing his usefulness to architectural history and historians until his death in 1969. Howard Dearstyne moved on from Williamsburg to a teaching career of two decades at the School of Architecture of the Illinois Institute of Technology. Mr. Dearstyne gave invaluable advice to the editor of Colonial Williamsburg publications, Thomas K. Ford, in bringing to fruition the present revision.

As the restoration of Virginia's colonial capital reaches its fiftieth anniversary in 1976, it seems most appropriate that this new edition of a remarkably long-lived publication can make its appearance as a part of Colonial Williamsburg's observance of the national bicentennial.

—Carlisle H. Humelsine
President

CONTENTS

The Virginia Planters' Capital

*"The moral influence of the large plantation . . .
fostered habits of self-reliance in individual men; it
assisted in promoting an intense love of liberty; it
strengthened the ties of family and kinship at the very
time that it cultivated the spirit of general hospital-
ity."*

—PHILIP A. BRUCE

WHEN THE FIRST settlers of Virginia landed at Jamestown, they found themselves in a most unfriendly environment; they were confronted by a mysterious wilderness, unfamiliar flora and fauna, and a strange and hostile race of men. In their struggle for survival in this New World, these early colonists had little opportunity to develop architecture of lasting significance. There was, however, the immediate need for shelter and protection. Carpenters and bricklayers were put to work, and houses soon sprang up within a wooden stockade. These first shelters were rough-hewn; one seventeenth-century writer considered them as devoid of architectural beauty as a barn, lacking both chimneys and partitions. Still later, even homes of prominent planters were often described as "simple and plain."

On the other hand, structures of considerable architectural pretension were soon planned along the James and York rivers. In Surry County, for example, the country seat known as Bacon's Castle was under construction within a half century of the landing at Jamestown. This Jacobean building, although small compared with English mansions, has an elaboration of detail in its doorways, mantels, and clustered chimneys that can be associated only with the "designed" house. Similar architectural ambitions were evident in churches such as St. Luke's near Smithfield, the church at Jamestown, and the early buttressed church at Middle Plantation. And, within one hundred years

of Jamestown's founding, the notable public buildings of Williamsburg—the Wren Building at the College of William and Mary, the Capitol, and the Governor's Palace—were either built or under construction.

PLANTATION SOCIETY

In colonial Virginia, architecture was developed to meet the requirements and tastes of a plantation society, a society in which social prestige and political power depended primarily on tobacco, "the Indian weed" which John Rolfe improved by crossbreeding. After the land was safe from Indian attack, and the woodlands sufficiently cleared, the broad fertile Tidewater was dotted with plantations, large and small, with their mansions and outbuildings. The broadleafed plant sustained a planter aristocracy which prided itself on its great estates, such as Westover, Berkeley, Carter's Grove, Tuckahoe, Brandon, Stratford, and Shirley.

Except for certain manufactured articles, which were imported from England, the planter became largely self-sufficient. The wealthy planter was master of a small village. The plantation house, with its numerous dependent buildings, was an expression of this remarkable community. At an appropriate distance from the mansion were the kitchen, smokehouse, dairy, storehouse, washhouse, coach house, and stable. There might even be a schoolhouse. Near

1

A Virginia tobacco wharf as depicted by a London artist to illustrate the famous
Fry-Jefferson map of the colony, first published in 1751. This redrawing by the late
Elmo Jones is used by courtesy of the Mariners Museum, Newport News.

the tobacco fields were the rude slave quarters. Timber for building was cut from the planter's own land and sawed by his own sawyers. Brick used in his mansion was molded, and burned in a kiln, from clay dug on his own plantation. Hogsheads in which tobacco was shipped were made in his cooper's shop. Shoes were fashioned in his own shoemaker's shop, out of leather provided by his tannery. At the smithy, the plantation's blacksmiths hammered out hardware, shod horses, and repaired farm implements and wagons.

The plantation house was patterned after English mansions, but was adapted to meet the needs of plantation life. Spacious, high-ceilinged rooms offered comfort in summer heat and were well suited for entertainment; for, if plantation life imposed its burden of cares, it also had its amenities. There was a constant interchange of visits among the plantations, which were rarely without guests. Philip Fithian, in 1773 tutor at Nomini Hall, the Westmoreland County home of Councilor Robert Carter, makes numerous references to balls, barbecues, billiards, card games, and other social events. Children of the planters acquired social graces early, and were usually given dancing lessons; Fithian, observing one lesson conducted by an exacting tutor, noted in his diary: "There were several Minuets danced with great ease and propriety; after which the whole company Joined in country-dances, and it was indeed beautiful to admiration, to see such a number of young persons, set off by dress to the best Advantage, moving easily, to the sound of well performed Music."

WILLIAMSBURG AS CAPITAL

Williamsburg itself was the political and social metropolis of this plantation gentry, and reflects this role in its architectural development. Because of the predominantly agricultural character of the colony, Williamsburg, unlike such populous trading marts as Boston, New York, or Philadelphia, resembled "a good Country Town in England"; its population (white and black included) probably never exceeded two thousand. Yet it served as the seat of government and as the cultural center for one of Britain's largest and most powerful colonies; its size belies its importance in shaping the American past. Its political significance is intimated in the Capitol; its prestige for the crown in the Governor's Palace; its cultural role in Bruton Church and in the Wren Building of the College of William and Mary.

The historical and architectural significance of Williamsburg is largely confined to its tenure as capital of Virginia, during the years 1699 to 1780. Settled in 1633 as an outpost against Indian attack, the spot was then called Middle Plantation. When the capital was moved to it in 1699 from Jamestown, six miles away, the town was renamed Williamsburg, in honor of King William III. In 1780, during a critical stage of the Revolutionary War, the capital was moved to Richmond, which was considered "more safe and central

than any other town situated on navigable water." Its mission fulfilled, Williamsburg fell into a decline. Its historic importance was to lie buried for a century and a half.

Despite the care with which colonial Williamsburg has been re-created, the modern visitor may have difficulty visualizing exactly what the town was like in the eighteenth century. In addition to seeing buildings, gardens, and costumed people, he needs some knowledge of its merchants and craftsmen, its political and cultural and religious leaders, its womenfolk, its children, and its servant population, both black and white. Williamsburg in the past was a living town; great care is taken today to make it a living museum in which visitors may both see and understand the significance of Virginia's small but important colonial capital.

"PUBLICK TIMES"

For most of the year, Williamsburg was a small college town and market place, but twice annually, during "publick times," the planters' capital sprang to life. It was then that the General Court met and often the General Assembly was also in session. A crowded social and political calendar attracted men of every

Carter's Grove, an eighteenth-century plantation near Williamsburg, restored and enlarged in 1929.

pocketbook and profession from all parts of the colony. The population of the town doubled almost overnight, and every available inn, tavern, and private house was packed to overflowing.

The most prominent persons of the colony came to Williamsburg at these times and often brought their families for the entertainments that were planned for the season. Officials and their wives attended elegant dinners and balls at the Governor's Palace, and at the taverns hosts and dancing masters offered assembly balls and suppers to all who cared to purchase tickets. Traveling theatrical troupes planned their best dramatic performances to coincide with public times and adjusted admission charges to attract all classes to seats in the boxes, the pit, or the gallery. Horse races, too, enlivened the scene with crowds of spectators closely packed along the sides of the track, enjoying their favorite sport.

Both to stimulate trade and to amuse the crowds, Williamsburg's fairs were scheduled to run for three days each spring and fall. A notice appearing in a *Virginia Gazette* of 1739 reveals their nature and objectives:

> WHEREAS TWO FAIRS are appointed to be held in this City . . . out of a laudable Design to encourage the Trade thereof, and to be a Means of promoting a general Commerce or Traffick among Persons that want to buy or sell, either the Product or Manufactures of the Country. . . .
>
> IT *is therefore Agreed upon, and Ordered,* That the following . . . shall be given as *Bounties.* . . .
>
> To the Person that brings most Horses to the said FAIR, and there offers them to Publick Sale . . . a Pistole. . . .
>
> To the Person that brings most Cows, Steers, or other horned Cattle . . . a Pistole shall be given. . . .
>
> AND for the *Entertainment* and *Diversion* of all Gentlemen and others, that shall resort thereto, the following PRIZES are given to be contended for . . . *viz.*
>
> A good Hat to be Cudgell'd for. . . .
>
> A Saddle of 40 *s.* Value, to be run for, once round the Mile Course, adjacent to this City. . . .
>
> A Pair of Silver Buckles, Value 20 *s.* to be run for by Men, from the *College* to the *Capitol.* . . .
>
> A Pair of Pumps to be danc'd for by Men.
>
> A handsome Firelock to be exercis'd for. . . .
>
> A Pig, with his Tail soap'd, to be run after. . . .

Fashionable head-dresses of 1780

TRADES AND CRAFTS

Williamsburg was not a large trading center, but its shopkeepers and craftsmen made the most of public times to display the finest goods produced in the colony and articles "after the newest fashion" imported from England. The latest creations in clothing and household furnishings often appeared in Williamsburg sooner than in out-of-the-way towns in England; planters had the latest London modes to choose from, and the shops did a thriving business.

Although never an important manufacturing city, Williamsburg at one time or another during the colonial period did produce furniture, candles, coaches, saddles and harness, jewelry, shoes, hosiery, and wigs. For the most part, these articles were purchased by townspeople. In its early days, particularly, Williamsburg depended almost completely on England for manufactured articles; the extent of this dependence, even as late as 1752, is suggested by a notice in the *Virginia Gazette* announcing the arrival of "A FRESH Cargoe of live human Hairs, all ready curl'd and well prepared by the best Hands in *London.*" With the passage of the Stamp Act and other restrictive measures, however, relations with England became more and more strained, imports declined, and home crafts and manufactures received increasing support and encouragement.

Typical of the response to such measures is a notice that appeared in the *Gazette* in 1769 requesting ladies and gentlemen to turn in their old gold and silver to

JAMES GEDDY,
GOLDSMITH,
NEAR THE CHURCH, WILLIAMSBURG,

HAS just imported from *London* a genteel assortment of PLATE and JEWELLERY; he has likewise on hand all sorts of country made GOLD and SILVERWORK, which he will sell at lower rates than usual.----Old SILVER taken in exchange for new work, at 7s. per ounce, and GOLD at 5l. 5s.----He repairs his own work, that fails in a reasonable time, without any expence to the purchaser. 4

Opposite, Bookbinder at Wor

James Geddy, goldsmith, "[who], as he has not imported any jewellery this season . . . flatters himself he will meet with encouragement." At Capitol Landing, a mile from town, a factory was established which announced that it was prepared to turn out cloth as good as could be woven in England. The introduction of the mulberry tree to Virginia in the hope of establishing a silk industry did not meet with the success expected, although a notice in the *Gazette* in 1775 reported that a certain Mr. Estave collected enough cocoons in a single year to produce one hundred pounds of silk fit for manufacture.

TYPOGRAPHIA.

AN

ODE,

ON

PRINTING.

Infcrib'd to the Honourable

WILLIAM GOOCH, Efq;

His Majefty's Lieutenant-Governor, and Commander in Chief of the Colony of *VIRGINIA.*

------------ Pleni funt omnes Libri, plenæ fapientum voces, plena Exemplorum vetuftas ; quæ jacerent in Tenebris omnia, nifi Literarum Lumen accederet.

Cic. Orat. pro Archia.

WILLIAMSBURG:

Printed by WILLIAM PARKS. M,DCC,XXX.

One of the first examples of printing in Virginia was published in 1730 by William Parks, founder of the *Virginia Gazette*. It was the earliest American appreciation of the press and was "occasion'd by the setting up a printing-press in Williamsburg."

No discussion of trades and crafts in Williamsburg would be complete which failed to mention William Parks and printing. Parks opened an office on Duke of Gloucester Street about 1730 and printed and sold many books, including William Stith's *The History of the First Discovery and Settlement of Virginia, The Whole Body of the Laws of Virginia, The Poor Planter's Physician, Poems by a Gentleman of Virginia,* and numerous other publications concerning religion, music, school subjects, and military tactics. Through his office and those of his successors, books and current London magazines were imported and sold. The first number of the *Virginia Gazette,* oldest newspaper in the colony, was issued by Parks in 1736. Less than ten years later, with the aid of Benjamin Franklin, Parks established a paper mill on the outskirts of Williamsburg, advertising that he desired "all Persons to save their old *Linen Rags,* for making Paper," adding that "As this is the first Mill of the Kind, that ever was erected in this Colony, and has cost a very considerable Sum of Money," he hoped "to meet with Encouragement suitable to so useful an Undertaking." Parks, who was a fine typographer and a skillful editor, has justly been called a dean among early American printers, and his influence on the culture of the city and colony was extensive.

CULTURE AND RELIGION

The presence in the town of the College of William and Mary, founded in 1693 and, after Harvard, the oldest college in the colonies, helped make Williamsburg the cultural center of Virginia. The relationship between the college and the colonial government was close; William and Mary was actually represented in the House of Burgesses, the only college in the colonies enjoying such a privilege. Students included Thomas Jefferson, Benjamin Harrison, James Monroe, John Tyler, John Marshall, Edmund Randolph, and others influential in America's formative years. Among distinguished faculty members was George Wythe, tutor of Jefferson and first professor of law at an American college.

The site of the college was ideal. The act of 1699, directing the development of Williamsburg, had reflected that "it will prove highly advantageous and beneficial to his Majesty's Royall Colledge of William & Mary to have the conveniences of a towne near the same." Located in the center of the social, cultural,

Household utensils in the Palace Kitchen. We note with admiration the grace and endurance of such homely objects as ladles, draining and skimming spoons, long-handled fireplace forks, molds, and skewers.

and political life of the colony, the college could offer students first-hand study of colonial society and government. Perhaps the largest debt owed to one man by the young college was due the Reverend James Blair, energetic and fiery Scottish clergyman who fought hard for its inception and became its first president. A notice in the London *Post Boy* in 1706 shows the rapidly growing reputation of the college: "Some . . . from Virginia tell us that the College which had been lately founded there . . . is so crowded with Students, that they begin to think of enlarging the College, for it seems divers from Pensilvania, Maryland, and Carolina send their Sons thither to be educated."

Virginia was fortunate in having a number of royal governors who were men of learning and who supported and encouraged the work of the college and the cultural life of Williamsburg. Among these were Governor Fauquier, greatly admired by Thomas Jefferson, and Lord Botetourt, in whose honor the Botetourt medals for scholarship have been awarded by the college continuously since that time. Even Governor Dunmore, later the object of the colonists' suspicion and hatred, was a sponsor of the Society for the Advancement of Useful Knowledge (1773), through which the founders hoped "to direct the Attention of their Countrymen to the Study of Nature, with a View

of multiplying the Advantages that may result from this Source of Improvement. . . . It is therefore the Intention of this Society to rescue from Oblivion every useful Essay."

Eighteenth-century Virginians loved and appreciated music; planters' children were expected to learn to sing or play some instrument. Many music teachers gave lessons in the town and toured the plantations to instruct in the violin, harpsichord, and pianoforte. Outstanding among these was Cuthbert Ogle, whose inventory of effects lists a fine collection of sonatas and concertos by English composers and many books of Handel's songs and oratorios. Psalmody was a part of services at Bruton Church. Fiddling contests were events at every fair, and home concerts were frequent. Jefferson joined with Governor Fauquier and others in impromptu chamber musicales at the Palace. Theatre patrons were often entertained between acts by performers on French horns, trumpets, and other instruments.

Between 1716 and 1718 William Levingston erected the first theatre in America on the east side of the Palace Green, proposing to present in this "good Substantial house commodious for Acting" comedies, "drolls," and other kinds of stage plays. Many of the productions were amateur. The *Virginia Gazette*, for

"The [Wren] Building is beautiful and commodious, being first modelled by Sir Christopher Wren, adapted to the Nature of the Country by the Gentlemen there. . . ."—Hugh Jones, 1724.

example, announced in 1736 the performance there of *The Tragedy of Cato* by the "young Gentlemen of the College" and other plays by the "Gentlemen and Ladies of this Country."

Although this pioneer venture at first met with hearty approval, and the playhouse was filled night after night, it was forced to close two decades later for financial reasons. A second playhouse was erected in 1751 near the Capitol. Here Lewis Hallam and his company from London made their American debut in *The Merchant of Venice.* Hallam announced that he had brought with him "Scenes, Cloaths and Decorations . . . all entirely new, extremely rich . . . excell'd by none in Beauty and Elegance, so that the Ladies and Gentlemen may depend on being entertain'd in as polite a Manner as at the Theatres in *London.*" Patrons of Hallam's theatre included many prominent colonists. George Washington was an enthusiastic playgoer, noting in his diary that he "Dined at the President's and went to the Play" or that he "Reach'd Williamsburg before Dinner, and went to the Play in the Afternoon."

Pulpit of Bruton Church. According to an early writer, Bruton was "adorned as the best Churches in London."

Doubtless one of the factors influencing the choice of Middle Plantation as the seat of government in Virginia was the presence there of Bruton Church. The church, a Gothic structure with buttresses, which had

The Reverend Mr. George Whitefield, impetuous Anglican priest who with the Wesleys began the Methodist movement, "arrived in December, 1739, at Williamsburg, and preached there in Bruton Church, producing great excitement." Portrait by John Wollaston; courtesy of the National Portrait Gallery, London.

been completed in 1683, was not adequate to serve as court church of the colony; and so a new church, the same building which stands today, was erected between 1711 and 1715 from plans furnished by Governor Spotswood, and became the center of religious life in the new capital. Here the governors came each Sunday to worship, as did the members of the Council and the House of Burgesses when in Williamsburg. The aristocracy of Williamsburg and near-by plantations assembled here to listen to the sermons and to display their best attire. The students of the college occupied a special gallery reserved for them.

The people of Williamsburg and the surrounding country sought spiritual guidance at Bruton Church in times of stress, as when periods of drought or epidemics of "distemper" visited the colony, or when the political situation became critical. In 1774, for example, when Parliament ordered the sealing of the port

By PERMISSION of the Honble *ROBERT DINWIDDIE,* Efq; His Majefty's Lieutenant-Governor, and Commander in Chief of the Colony and Dominion of *Virginia.*

By a Company of COMEDIANS, *from* LONDON, *At the* THEATRE *in* WILLIAMSBURG, On *Friday* next, being the 15th of *September,* will be prefented, A PLAY, Call'd,

THE
MERCHANT of *VENICE.*

(Written by *Shakefpear.*)

The Part of *ANTONIO* (the MERCHANT) to be perform'd by
Mr. CLARKSON.

GRATIANO, by Mr. SINGLETON,
Lorenzo, (with Songs in Character) by Mr. ADCOCK.
The Part of *BASSANIO* to be perform'd by
Mr. RIGBY.

Duke, by Mr. Wynell.
Salanio, by Mr. Herbert. *good name*
The Part of *LAUNCELOT,* by Mr. HALLAM.
And the Part of *SHYLOCK,* (the JEW) to be perform'd by
Mr. MALONE.

The Part of *NERISSA,* by Mrs. ADCOCK,
Jeffica, by Mrs. Rigby.
And the Part of *PORTIA,* to be perform'd by
Mrs. HALLAM.

With a new occafional PROLOGUE.
To which will be added, a FARCE, call'd,
The ANATOMIST:
OR,
SHAM DOCTOR.

The Part of *Monfieur le Medecin,* by
Mr. RIGBY.

And the Part of *BEATRICE,* by Mrs. ADCOCK.
*** No Perfon, whatfoever, to be admitted behind the Scenes.
BOXES, 7s. 6d. PIT and BALCONIES, 5s. 9d. GALLERY, 3s. 9d.
To begin at Six o'Clock.

Vivat Rex.

of Boston, the House of Burgesses set aside June 1 as a day of fasting, humiliation, and prayer. On that day, the members of the House proceeded to the church in a body "to implore the divine interposition, for averting the heavy Calamity which threatens destruction to our Civil Rights, and the Evils of civil War." Washington wrote in his diary that he "Went to [Bruton] Church and fasted all day."

Life in eighteenth-century Williamsburg followed closely the cultural patterns of the mother country. Under the influence of new forces at work in a new land, however, colonial Virginians moved steadily toward new patterns; they became less English and more distinctly citizens of Virginia and of the new nation in the making. The life and customs of the country dictated the manner of its architecture. Although this architecture was based originally on the mode of building already established in eighteenth-century England, it was "adapted to the Nature of the Country" by the local builders and craftsmen and became definitely Virginian. It changed as life in the colony changed and varied from place to place under the influence of local conditions; thus Williamsburg, too, developed an architecture of its own. The architects of the twentieth-century restoration sought to recapture that local individuality; in their own words "[it was] the essence of restoration philosophy so to comprehend the eighteenth century in England and so to study its variations in the colonies, especially Virginia, that the Georgian mode and manner were eventually translated into a vernacular *specifically of Williamsburg.*"

Tobacco plant (*Nicotiana tabacum*) from a 1764 manuscript on tobacco cultivation by Nicholas José Rapun. Courtesy of the Arents Collection, New York Public Library, the Astor, Lenox, and Tilden Foundations.

Buildings and Builders of Williamsburg

"Williamsburg, at the Revolution, was a town of beauty and of architectural significance; its major buildings were milestones in the history of American style, its Palace Garden perhaps the most beautiful in America."

—FISKE KIMBALL

IN THE YEAR 1759 the traveler Andrew Burnaby graphically described Williamsburg as a place for "agreeable residence." He observed that the town was "regularly laid out in parallel streets, intersected by others at right angles; [it] has a handsome square in the center, through which runs the principal street, one of the most spacious in North-America. . . . At the ends of this street are two public buildings, the college and the capitol, and . . . the whole makes a handsome appearance." This "handsome appearance" owed much to careful town planning, in which principles still in use today were followed. The site selected was an eminence between two rivers in a region reasonably free from the pestilential dampness that had made Jamestown so unhealthful.

THE TOWN PLAN

The character of the new town at Middle Plantation was established in a plan provided in 1699 by Governor Francis Nicholson, who soon afterward was to boast of being "the Founder of a new City." He laid out the streets and opened squares and located the proposed public buildings. What proved to be his most notable achievement was the stipulation that each house lot should be one-half acre in size. It was furthermore Nicholson's view that each person should have his own dwelling place, with a sufficient quantity of ground for his house, his garden, and orchard. The act directing the building of Williamsburg, a measure of importance in the history of modern town planning,

specified "that two hundred & twenty Acres . . . be . . . sett a part for ground on which the said City shall be built and erected according to the form and manner laid downe in the said draught or plott."

Analysis of the plan itself underscores the significance of the document. The plot for each home builder was precisely specified; comments were even made on the design of the houses, and their set-back from the street was determined. In several respects the regulations read like a zoning ordinance of a twentieth-century suburban community:

"The Said City of Williamsburgh shall be laid out and proportioned into halfe Acres every of Which halfe Acre shall be a distinct lott of ground to be built upon in manner and forme as is hereafter expressed that is to say that whosoever shall build in the maine Street of the said City of Williamsburgh as laid out in the aforesaid draught or Plott shall not build a house less than tenn foot pitch [meaning from ground floor to the second floor] and the front of each house shall come within Six foot of the street and not nearer and that the houses in the Severall lots in the Said main street shall front a like."

These regulations were made in 1699, when other cities in the American colonies were also being planned—Charleston, for example, in 1672, and Philadelphia in 1682, though neither had a plan conceived in so comprehensive or so grand a manner.

This was a time of new ideas in town planning. In

The kitchen of the St. George Tucker House, distinguished by its massive chimney.

the proposed layout for Williamsburg, several novel principles were incorporated that may well have been suggested by the schemes for the rebuilding of London following the Great Fire of 1666. In the plan of Williamsburg, as proposed by Governor Nicholson, Duke of Gloucester Street was made a wide esplanade, skillfully terminated by the Capitol at one end and by the college at the other. Comparing this for a moment with the unrealized plan for the rebuilding of London prepared by Sir Christopher Wren, the observer will note similar vistas that end with churches and public

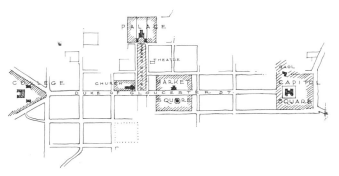

The college is at one end of Duke of Gloucester Street, the Capitol at the other. At a right angle to this street is Palace Green, terminated by the Palace.

buildings. Similarities in the width of streets were also marked. Duke of Gloucester Street was to be six poles, or ninety-nine feet, in width. Wren had called for ninety feet as the proposed width of the three principal streets of London. In the plan of John Evelyn, a farsighted English amateur architect who had hoped to rebuild London on a more orderly and spacious scale, the width of the main avenues had been specified as one hundred feet.

The Williamsburg scheme is climaxed by placing the Governor's Palace as a terminus facing a long and wide grassy plot. This approach to the Palace is given additional incisiveness and interest by flanking the grassy area with catalpa trees.

THE WILLIAMSBURG HOUSE

The half-acre plot specified for each Williamsburg house was the formula that gave an entirely new aspect to the settlement on the peninsula. Free-standing houses were built, with a garden and orchard space. The spacious lots were soon dotted with outbuildings, all having a design related to the main house and to the gardens. This was decidedly unlike the cramped

quarters of the narrow and medieval row-housing at Jamestown. Whereas the size of Jamestown was re-

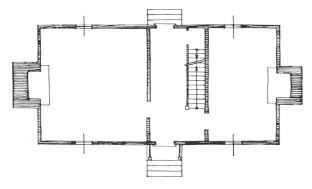

Bracken House. Early form of house plan, "one room deep," having a projecting chimney at each end. In some instances there was no central hallway, but stairs were within one of the rooms.

stricted by its peninsula site, Governor Nicholson's new town could spread out toward either the York River or the James.

One type of house which in time came to be characteristic of Williamsburg was a story and a half in height with a steep shingled roof, suggesting to one observer the appearance of "an inverted ship with ridged hull in the air." This house usually had a great chimney of brick at one or both ends, and its windows, placed on

Bracken House. A typical Williamsburg house, one story and a half in height, having a steep roof in the form of an A.

each side of a doorway, were often spaced with Vitruvian regularity. Dormers gave life to the roof.

Hugh Jones, in *The Present State of Virginia,* describes Williamsburg as it appeared in the years 1721 through 1724. "Here," he says, "as in other Parts, they build with Brick, but most commonly with Timber lined with Cieling, and cased with feather-edged Plank, painted with white Lead and Oil, covered with Shingles of *Cedar,* &c. tarr'd over at first; with a Passage generally through the Middle of the House for an Air-Draught in Summer." Governor Berkeley's house at Green Spring, two miles from Jamestown, was, according to the historian Bruce, described by a contemporary as having a "wide hall characteristic of all the larger dwellings in Virginia at this time. . . . The wideness of the hall was for the purpose of obtaining the fullest ventilation, the climate of this part of the Colony in the warm season being oppressive and unwholesome."

The house types of Williamsburg are in some respects local or indigenous to Virginia. All are moderate in size, yet comfortable and commodious. Their architecture is of a practical sort, without ornament or pretense, and their exteriors are mostly free from columns or other evidences of "the orders of architecture." With the single exception of the Governor's Palace, none of them recalls the academic grandeur of plantation mansions such as Westover, Shirley, or Rosewell. It is this simple type of house to which Isaac Ware refers in his *Complete Body of Architecture* (1756), and which, he says, appeals to the man in the country, who may be desirous of building "without columns, or other expensive decorations."

Although altered somewhat from decade to decade, three general plan types of Williamsburg houses of the

Gambrel roof with steep lower slope (Tayloe House), devised so as to obtain greater floor area within the roof.

eighteenth century may be identified and described. The first may be called the "one-room-deep" plan, with a hallway at its center and a room at either side. Tidewater Virginia had many such houses, a type rarely found in New England. The room arrangement apparently grew out of the seventeenth-century dwelling, "built of wood, yet contrived so delightful, that your ordinary houses in England are not so handsome." The plan illustration of the Bracken House reproduced on the previous page shows the rooms flanking the hallway to be of unequal width. The number of windows on either side of the doorway sometimes varies. This type of house had a chimney, usually an outside chimney, at one or both ends of the building.

A second type became popular near the middle of the eighteenth century: the "two-room-deep" plan, with a side hall. The Orrell, Tayloe, and William Lightfoot houses are among several Williamsburg examples of this one-sided plan. The front room, often designated "the parlour," was usually almost square and had a corner fireplace as did also the back room. The chimney was contained within the wall and one stack of flues served the two rooms. The corner fireplace was an innovation of the time of William and

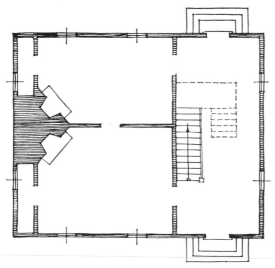

"Two-room-deep" plan with side hallway (Tayloe House).

Mary. John Evelyn speaks of it disdainfully in 1692, saying that "This plan of placing fireplaces in the corner of rooms has come into fashion . . . I predict that

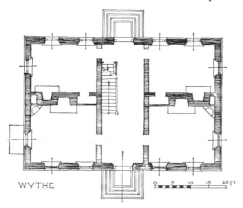

WYTHE   0 5 10 15 20 FT

The Wythe House. Third plan type, two rooms deep with center hall.

it will spoil many noble houses and rooms if followed. It does only well in very small and trifling rooms." It was, however, economical to construct, and the added heat reflected into the room because of the angle of

the walls made it efficient. Finally, as one writer says, "it offers a more prominent position for a painting"!

A third and much more spacious type of Williamsburg house was also two rooms in depth, but with a center hall and chimneys built within the area of the plan. The Governor's Palace is based on this arrangement, as are also the George Wythe, Robert Carter, and Lightfoot plans, and that of the President's House at the college. Most houses of this type have four rooms on each floor. The Robert Carter House is exceptional in having, with its one stairway, a second hall at the corner.

MATERIALS

For the small house, wood framing faced with weatherboarding continued to be the common construction method in the Virginia colony throughout the eighteenth century. The popularity of wood is ascribed to a contemporary prejudice that houses with brick walls were damp and consequently less wholesome. Jefferson, writing of construction in Virginia in

The front portion of the Quarter, 16 feet deep by 24 feet wide, suggests the original form of some early Williamsburg houses. This basic dimension may still be seen in many outbuildings.

Thomas Mott Shaw

Brickmaking in Williamsburg in the colonial manner: mixing the clay by mule power and a workman filling the brick molds.

Old colonial brickwork of the Public Records Office, showing texture of brick and glazed headers.

1784, notes that "private buildings are very rarely constructed of brick or stone; much the greater portion being of scantling and boards, plastered with lime." Williamsburg, however, had its fair share of brick buildings, showing usually a traditional use of English bond below the water table and Flemish bond above. English bond can readily be recognized by the surface pattern made up of a row of "header" bricks placed over a row of "stretchers." Flemish bond has alternating headers and stretchers over the entire wall surface. Madame Knight, a noted traveler of the period, remarked on the appearance of Flemish bond in New York: "Bricks in some of the houses are of divers colors and laid in checkers." Diamond patterns sometimes supplement the checkers on the eastern shore of Virginia and in Princess Anne County (now merged into Virginia Beach). One authority, writing in the early part of the nineteenth century, thus appraised the two methods: "Flemish bond is deemed the neatest and most beautiful, but is attended with a great deal of inconvenience in the execution, and in most cases does not unite the parts of a wall with the same degree of firmness as the English bond."

Bricks used for buildings of the town were burned on or near the site and were laid in a coarse oystershell lime mortar. The gray-green glaze seen on some headers was imparted by burning the bricks in a kiln fired with oakwood. Only those bricks nearest the heat acquired the glazed surface. The use of bricks rubbed down to a smooth surface or to a molded profile was a favorite means of imparting finish to a building. The rubbing was done with sharp sand on a piece of millstone or by rubbing two bricks together. Most of the colonial brick buildings in Williamsburg have rubbed brick for arches, water tables, and string-courses, and at the corners of their walls and chimneys. The finest example of original rubbed moldings is that in the pediment edge of the entrance doorway of the Public Records Office, near the Capitol. The versatility of the artisans who produced these and the moldings of the chimney tops is one of the most striking achievements of this age of craftsmanship.

The controversial theory that brick sizes can be used to determine the age of a building receives little support in Williamsburg, where a wide variety of sizes occurs. Bricks of largest dimensions appear in brick walls and pavements. The statute bricks of England, by act of Parliament, 1776, were 2 1/2 by 4 by 9 inches;

The Public Records Office, built after the Capitol burned in 1747, housed the secretary of the colony and his papers in fireproof security. The molded brick pediment and projecting pilasters of the doorway closely resemble those of nearby Carter's Grove.

this can be compared with an earlier statute brick of 1685, 2 1/4 by 4 1/4 by 8 3/4 inches. These British statute sizes did have their echo in the Virginia colony, however. The bricks for a wall around St. Peter's Church, New Kent County, were in 1719 specified to be "according to the Statute something Less then Nine Inches in Length, two Inches and one quarter thick, and four Inches and one quarter Wide."

Numerous studies of masonry building in America before the Revolution report that brick was brought from England as ballast. It has become customary to refute this claim. Certainly, most building sites in town and on plantations were the scene of brick burning, and clay suitable for brick was found everywhere in tidewater Virginia. There does exist, however, a reasonable basis to believe that brick occasionally was imported into the Virginia colony as ballast. The practice is implied by an act of October 1748, "That nothing herein contained shall be construed to prohibit or restrain the master of any ship or other vessel, bringing limestone, chalk, bricks, or stone for building, to lade or put the same on board any other vessel, in order to be carried or transported to any place he shall think fit."

Outside wood walls of dwellings and dairy buildings were sometimes filled with partly burned bricks, a construction vastly superior as insulation to ordinary lathing and plastering on wood frame and also more fireproof. The outer walls of the John Blair House and a few others were found to be of this type. A recommendation was made in the colonies that "Partitions [of wood] between rooms . . . might be superseded, for greater security, by partitions of 4 inch brick walls, vulgarly called 'bricknogging'. . . . Many houses have been burned by servants sticking candles against wooden partitions."

THE VIRGINIA CHIMNEY

The huge outside house chimneys so familiar in the Williamsburg landscape appear to be typical of tidewater Virginia, although not restricted to the colony. They derive from earlier examples in England and are associated there with the seventeenth century. Following the Great Fire of 1666, chimney stacks for London were regulated "within the wall face."

The characteristic Virginia chimney is of brick, broad at the base so as to give a roomy fireplace within, sloping at the sides to a smaller upper shaft. Because of the need to make domestic fires safe, the chimney top rises past the gable of the house without coming into contact with shingles or other woodwork. This chimney form may have followed closely that of the original wood-framed or "catted" chimney. The wooden prototypes appear to have been common in early days. Samuel Groome in 1683 wrote one of the Proprietors in London that his chimney was "made with timber and clay as the manner of this country is to build." Examples of wood-frame chimneys continued to be built for occasional outbuildings in Virginia until the end of the nineteenth century.

Outside brick chimney of the Todd House near Fredericksburg. The sloping flanks indicate the position of the fireplaces within.

WILLIAMSBURG INFLUENCE

Paralleling the political and social prestige of Williamsburg, its architecture too had a wide influence. As early as 1665, long before the town was established, a church was ordered built in Middlesex County "according to the Modall of the Middle-plantacoñ Church in all Respects." Later, in 1719, when an enclosing wall and gates were voted for St. Peter's Church in New Kent County, the instructions to the builder were for "Handsom Gates made after the fform of Iron Gates . . . with a hollow Spire a Top. . . . [The] Wall to be in all Respects as well Done as the Capitol wall in Williams: Burgh." The town of Hanover Court House at mid-century specified that its new powder magazine follow in design the Magazine at Williamsburg. It is known also that builders living in Williamsburg—Morris, Cary, Minetree, and others—were commissioned to construct plantation houses in the surrounding country.

Catted chimney of Virginia cabin. The "cats" were rolls of straw and clay worked together and laid between the posts. Notched log construction was never characteristic of tidewater Virginia.

Opposite, chimney of the James Anderson Kitchen. The broad base of kitchen chimneys in Williamsburg sometimes enclosed an oven as well as a fireplace.

The ornamental cupola of the Capitol was the first of its kind in colonial America.

BUILDING THE CAPITOL AND PALACE

An act of June 7, 1699, directed the building of the Capitol in Williamsburg. That structure was a notable landmark in colonial American architecture, partly because it was one of the first public buildings of size erected in the colonies, and partly because it gave the first evidence of transition from the essential medievalism of Bacon's Castle to what was to become the classical manner of eighteenth-century Virginia. Its H plan suggests the past, but externally the appearance is classical, with round-headed sash windows and doors, bracketed cornice, balconies, and cupola.

The act prescribed that the building "Shall be made in the forme and figure H . . . the foundation . . . shall be four Bricks thick . . . the length of each Side or parte . . . shall be seventy five foot . . . one end of each Part or Side of Which Shall be . . . Semi-circular and the lower rooms at the . . . end fifty foot long." A "handsome Staire Case" is specified, and there were to be "great folding gates to each Porch of Six foot breadth . . . the windows to each Story of the Said building Shall be Sash windows and . . . the roofe Shall be a hip roof with Dormand windows." In the middle of the roof there was to be "a Cupulo to surmount the rest of the building Which Shall have a Clock placed in it and on the top of the Said Cupulo Shall be put a flag upon occasion."

Drawings of a simple nature were used by the builders to supplement this detailed description. Succinct but positive reference is made to a "Draught" and "Modell of the said Capitoll." Henry Cary, a builder known also as "Carpenter" and "Overseer," was employed upon his own petition to superintend the work. Shortly afterward the committee for the building authorized "the said Henry Cary to agree with any Capeable pson to make 500000 bricks for the Capitol." Construction progressed so that by July 20, 1703, "That parte that the Corte sits in is Compleatly finnished on the outside except the Balcony over the Grate doore Comming in on the west side & the lower flower are finished for that the Corte sate there in Aprill last."

The instructions for building were not complete in the original act, and "Further Directions in Building the Capitoll" were incorporated in a supplemental act of August 1701. It would therefore appear that the design conception for the building was probably not complete at the outset; alterations were made from time to time, and Cary made many suggestions during the course of building.

Construction of the governor's house followed, as authorized in 1706. Cary was again asked to direct construction, "to inspect, oversee, and provide for the building aforesaid, with full power to begin, carry on, and finish the same." This building advanced more slowly than the Capitol, in part because of difficulties in obtaining funds. On November 24, 1710, Cary was forced to petition the General Assembly for his full pay of one hundred pounds per annum, owed to him as "Overseer of the building." He declared that the money originally appropriated had long been exhausted, but that he felt himself under obligation to take care of and protect the building in its incompleted condition; he complained that he had been put to considerable expense, and to save himself from ruin had broken up housekeeping at his own plantation and moved his family to the unfinished building, "all of which was very prejudicial."

Governor Spotswood finally brought the building to completion, but not until about 1720. As a reward for his efforts, after rumors of mismanagement, the burgesses charged him with "lavishing away the Country's Funds." From this circumstance, and because of elaborate later additions, the house of the governor came to be known as the "Governor's Palace."

THE ARCHITECT IN VIRGINIA

An architect during the first part of the eighteenth century was known as a "Master Workman; in a Building . . . he who designs the Model, or draws the Plot, Plan, or Draught . . . [and] whose Business it is to consider the whole Manner and Method of the Building." In many instances he was a carpenter or a bricklayer. It is clear that the ability to produce a "draught" was also the accomplishment of an educated gentleman. As an instance, Henry Cary is spoken of as a "Gentleman" as well as "Overseer." Virginia had no practicing architects until William Buckland arrived in 1755 to supervise the building of George Mason's Gunston Hall. Other architects were gifted amateurs; those active in Williamsburg include Thomas Jefferson and Richard Taliaferro. Curiously, however, not a single building of Williamsburg of the eighteenth cen-

The governor's house was described by a traveler as large, commodious, and handsome.

tury can be assigned with documentary proof to an architect as designer.

In 1772, Jefferson made plans for the completion of the Wren Building as it had been planned, a rectangular building enclosing a quadrangle or court. Part of the foundation for the addition was actually laid before the Revolution put a stop to building operations. Later he drew plans for remodeling the Palace, which, he said, "is capable of being made an elegant seat." These plans also came to nothing, because the building burned in 1781.

THE USE OF HANDBOOKS

The working details used by builders of the early eighteenth century in composing their building de-

signs were obtained from builders' handbooks of which many had been published in London before

To be LET, on Wednesday the 4th of January next, if fair, otherwise next fair day,
THE BUILDING of a STEEPLE to Williamsburg church. All Gentlemen that incline to undertake the same are desired to attend that day at the said church with proper plans, and a just estimate to each plan,
JOHN PIERCE, } Church-
WILLIAM EATON, } Wardens.

The functions of the colonial architect were exercised by gentlemen and builders called "undertakers." The advertisement above is from the *Virginia Gazette* of December 15, 1768.

The exterior design of a typical Williamsburg house, such as the Alexander Craig House, was a development of the local carpenter and mason. But interior features such as cornices, doors, windows, and chimney details, were copied from builders' handbooks.

1700. These early manuals warrant description. The handbooks informed the builders how to frame a wall or roof, how to produce designs of windows, doorways, balconies, fireplaces, and cornices. A minimum of instruction was given, however, on the "orders of architecture," and no complete designs for buildings were included. Yet with this limited assistance the craftsmen built the Capitol, Palace, and many other early eighteenth-century Williamsburg buildings.

Later, actual designs of buildings were incorporated in more comprehensive publications by such men as James Gibbs, Isaac Ware, William Halfpenny, and Robert Morris. These writer-architects were producers of designs which, to quote Gibbs in 1728, "would be of use to such Gentlemen as might be concerned in Building, especially in the remote parts of the Country, where little or no assistance for Designs can be procured."

Books on architecture were frequently included on the library lists of residents of Williamsburg. Maurice Evington, a carpenter-builder, advertised in the *Virginia Gazette* in 1779, the sale of "12 or 15 books of architecture, by the latest and best authors in *Britain*, viz *Swan, Pain, Langley, Halfpenny,* &c. &c." George Wythe, with a more scholarly interest, wrote abroad for a copy of Vitruvius in Latin, having the advice of Thomas Jefferson that "the edition of Vitruvius . . . with commentaries by Ticinus . . . is best."

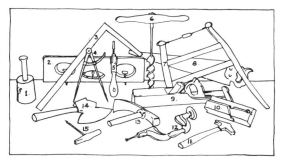

Examples of the principal items in the carpenter's equipment are illustrated below, with their numbers shown at right. For each named example there were many varieties adapted to special uses. Of planes alone, the carpenter often owned thirty or more. Many of these tools were made by the carpenter or by the local blacksmith. 1. Mallet. 2. Adjustable Level. 3. Square. 4. Compass. 5. Screw Driver (not used much before 1800). 6. Auger. 7. Buck Saw. 8. Hand Saw. 9. Jackplane. 10. Molding Plane. 11. Claw Hammer. 12. Brace. 13. Adze. 14. Hatchet. 15. Gimlet.

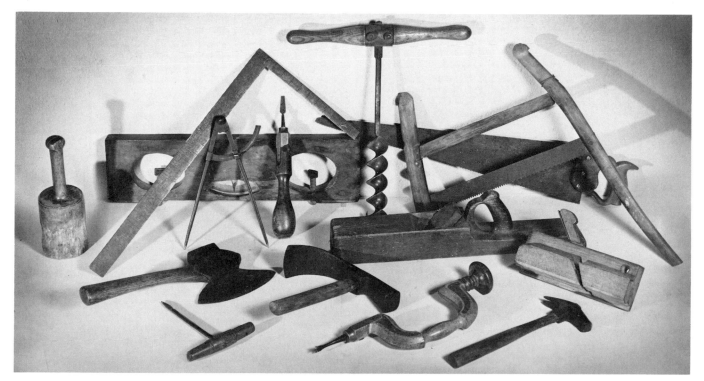

The Manner of Furnishings

"How much more agreeable it is to sit in the midst of old furniture . . . which [has] come down from other generations, than amid that which was just brought from the Cabinetmaker's, smelling of varnish, like a coffin!"

—Henry David Thoreau

THE COLONISTS in eighteenth-century Virginia made a deliberate effort to create and maintain an environment comparable to that of England. They kept informed of the latest decorative practices in the mother country and followed them in the treatment of the interiors of their homes and public buildings. Many of the materials for finishing and furnishing these were imported from England, and colonial artisans were in large part trained there. Numerous travelers were struck by the marked similarity of the appointments of Virginia and English houses; a comment made by one visitor about 1755 concerning an ordinary in Leedstown, Virginia, may be taken as typical. "The chairs, Tables, &c of the Room I was conducted into, was all of Mahogany, and so stuft with fine large glaized Copper Plate Prints: That I almost fancied myself in Jeffriess' [in London]."

WALLS, CEILINGS, AND FLOORS

The interior walls of Williamsburg buildings of the eighteenth century were usually plastered, use being made of oyster-shell lime, river sand, and animal hair. The plaster was commonly whitewashed.

Full-length wainscoting or paneling, originally a protection against damp walls, was sometimes used in Williamsburg homes, as in the Peyton Randolph House, but it was more often employed in public buildings such as the Capitol and the Palace or in the larger mansions of plantation owners. A builder's dictionary of 1774 defines wainscot as "the timber work that serves to line the walls of a room, being usually made in pannels, and painted, to serve instead of hangings." In Williamsburg, the wainscot was customarily of local pine.

A "dwarf" wainscot or dado, carried to a height of from three to five feet from the floor, was more common in both private and public buildings. In some cases where the dado is used, special emphasis is given the fireplace by carrying paneling above it to the ceiling. A fine example of such treatment may be seen on the east wall of the living room of the Brush-Everard House, where also a chair-height wainscot has remained in place since its original installation in the eighteenth century.

A still more frequent wall treatment is that in which paneling is completely dispensed with, leaving only the wood base and cornice and a heavy, waisthigh protective molding known as a chair rail. A variety of wall treatments might often be found within a single building; for example, there was ample precedent in the reconstructed Capitol for the use of ceiling-height

Opposite, a common room in Wetherburn's Tavern.

wainscoting in the Council Chamber and the Court Room, a dado in the House of Burgesses, and a chair rail only in certain committee rooms.

An eighteenth-century architect-builder, in a discussion of English wall treatments that applies equally

1

well to Virginia, states that the rooms "were commonly wainscoted quite up to the ceiling, and terminated by a cornice; but later the custom is to carry it only up chair high . . . [whereas] the rest of the wall is covered with flowered paper, which is very cheap

and beautiful, or else it is finished with stucco covered with hanging; to prevent the paper being spoiled by the dampness of the wall, it is pasted on thin cloth, and fixed in frames."

Wallpapers became fashionable in the latter part of the eighteenth century as a substitute for whitewashed and paneled walls and because of a desire for added enrichment. The mode at one period favored Chinese designs. The *Virginia Gazette* of December 28,

Facsimile of early wallpaper from the Brush-Everard House.

Early eighteenth-century damask at Colonial Williamsburg.

1769, carried an advertisement that "JOSEPH KIDD, *Upholsterer, in Williamsburg,* HANGS rooms with paper or damask, stuffs sophas, couches, and chairs, in the neatest manner, makes all sorts of bed furniture, window curtains, and matrasses, and fits carpets to any room with the greatest exactness. . . . He also undertakes all sorts of HOUSE PAINTING, GILDING, and GLAZING; and

2   3   4   5

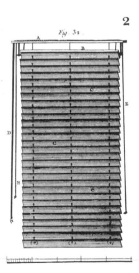

paints floor cloths, chimney boards, and signs, according to directions."

Records show that wallpaper was used in the Palace. In a letter written on April 15, 1771, to Samuel Athawes, Robert Beverley, referring to the ballroom, states that "L^d. B. [Lord Botetourt] had hung a room with plain blue paper & border'd it with a narrow stripe of gilt Leather." When the Palace interiors were restored, the walls of the supper room were covered with eighteenth-century paper painted in the Chinese manner, since Chinese patterns were in vogue in England at the time the wing containing this room was added. The upper middle room was hung with tooled and gilt Spanish Morocco leather similar to that mentioned in the journals of the Virginia Council. Damask hangings were a mark of interior elegance that apparently graced fewer Williamsburg homes than did wallpaper. In the Robert Carter House on Palace Green, however, wood strips used to attach the fabric still remain embedded in the plaster walls of certain rooms.

Casement windows with leaded glass were the prevailing window type in Virginia throughout the seventeenth century, and continued in use until well into the eighteenth century. Meanwhile, the vertical-sliding "guillotine" window came into favor and soon became the dominant type. Glazing was customary but, because of the expense of imported English glass, not universal. Basement windows had wood frames with square bars, but no provision for glazing, since the damp climate made circulation of air beneath the house a necessary precaution against mold and the rotting of timbers. Window weights of lead, with pulleys, were introduced early in the century although

ordinarily only the lower sash was made to operate. The common type of sash window throughout the eighteenth century was, however, without sash weights.

Outside shutters were used on wood-frame structures, whereas in brick houses and public buildings the deep reveals permitted the use of inside or wainscot shutters which folded against the jambs. Venetian blinds were introduced into Virginia after the middle of the eighteenth century. The *Virginia Gazette* in 1770 noted that Joshua Kendall, house carpenter and joiner, "BEGS leave to inform the Public that he . . . makes the best and newest invented *Venetian* SUN BLINDS for windows, that move to any position so as to give different lights, they screen from the scorching rays of the sun, draw up as a curtain, prevent being overlooked, give a cool refreshing air in hot weather, and are the greatest preservatives of furniture of any thing of the kind ever invented."

Windows were hung with draperies or curtains of damask, chintz, calico, printed linen, linsey-woolsey, or like materials. In bedchambers these usually matched the curtains of the bed.

Most Virginia rooms of the eighteenth century had a fireplace, since this was virtually the only means of heating at the time. By the latter part of the century a few stoves existed, and one example, the "Botetourt Stove," a cast-iron "ventilating type" which was given to the House of Burgesses and probably stood at one time in the Palace, can still be seen in Williamsburg. The fireplace was usually centered on the side or end

1. "Dwarf" wainscot, and paneled mantel facing of arched fireplace, Market Square Tavern. 2. Eighteenth-century drawing of Venetian blind (Diderot), 1765. 3. Operation of Venetian blind, window of Chowning's Tavern. 4. Bedroom of the Wythe House, showing eighteenth-century white cotton counterpane and an armchair upholstered in English crewelwork. 5. Paneling of upper passage in the Peyton Randolph House. 6. The Botetourt Stove, "the newly invented warming machine" considered by its inventor "as a masterpiece not to be equalled in all Europe."

wall of the room. Corner fireplaces, however, were more frequent in Williamsburg and Virginia than elsewhere in the colonies. Typically these corner fireplaces were built back-to-back in adjoining rooms, a single chimney serving the pair. Fireplace openings were large at the beginning of the century, tending later to decrease in size both because of the growing scarcity of wood and because improvements in their construction made them more efficient. The openings were spanned by a beam of heavy oak or by a brick arch until the time of the Revolution, after which the iron lintel gradually became common.

Stone for paving and mantels had to be brought to Williamsburg from England or other parts of Virginia and the colonies, since, with the exception of coarse marl rock which was only occasionally used for building, there was none native to the peninsula. William Byrd in 1732 recommended the quarrying of a "white stone" found near Fredericksburg, "appearing to be as fair and fine grained as that of Portland." This stone was used in Williamsburg and elsewhere in Virginia. Marbles and other stones for mantels were not confined to more pretentious buildings like the Palace but were also fairly common in private houses. The ledger of Humphrey Harwood, a Williamsburg carpenter-mason, records the following bill to Mrs. Betty Randolph, the widow of Peyton Randolph: "Decr. 2 [1778] To Repairing marble Chimney Piece 12/ [shillings]," and in 1790 occurs this entry in the account of John Blair, Esq.: "To setting up 2 grates (one very large)—taking down the marble-mantel-piece and taking up the Hearth—& relaying them 18/." The marble mantels found today in the Peyton Randolph and John Blair houses, it is believed, are the very ones mentioned in Harwood's account book.

Most mantel facings were of wood, and they were sometimes incorporated into the paneling of the room or combined with overmantels. The woodwork was separated from the fireplace opening by a "frame" of plastered brick or—in a number of Williamsburg homes—of imported delftware tiles. A hearth of brick or, quite frequently, English Purbeck or Portland stone, was provided.

Exposed beam ceilings had prevailed in the colony throughout the seventeenth century, but by the close of the first quarter of the eighteenth century ceilings of residences in Williamsburg were almost without exception lathed and plastered, for, as is noted in *The*

1

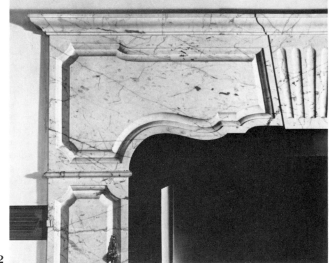

2

3

1. Eighteenth-century paneled wood mantel, John Blair house. The plastered brick frame and curved back of the fireplace are typical early details. 2. Marble mantel reproduction, George Wythe House. 3. Original marble mantel, east room of the Peyton Randolph House.

Opposite page, examples of colonial glassware.

Builder's Dictionary of 1734, experience revealed that "The Plaistered Ceilings so much used in England, beyond all other Countries, make by their whiteness the Rooms so much Lightsomer, and are excellent against raging Fires. They stop the Passage of the Dust, and lessen the noise over head; and in Summertime the Air of a Room is something the cooler for them, and in the Winter something the Warmer, because it keeps out cold Air better than the Board-floors alone can do."

The use of stone floors was restricted to public buildings; the Purbeck stone of the Capitol and Palace is notable. Brick and brickbat floors and pounded clay

THE College of WILLIAM & MARY has been lately cleaned, and will be immediately plaſtered and white-waſhed, to render it fit for the Reception of the Profeſſors, Students, Grammar Scholars, and Servants; and the ſeveral Schools will be opened at the Beginning of Trinity Term, namely, on *Monday* the 17th of next Month. (4)   EMMANUEL JONES, Clk.

were commonly found in kitchens and other dependencies. Aside from this, however, flooring was universally of local yellow pine, usually 1 1/4 inches thick, from 5- to 10-inch widths in edge grain, laid without underflooring, and generally face-nailed.

Rugs, as we speak of them today, were used sparingly on these floors, but English and Oriental types, and needlepoint, were employed. Until almost the middle of the eighteenth century carpets mentioned in records were used primarily as coverings for tables and bureaus; the turkey carpet specified for the table of the Council Chamber of the Capitol is a conspicuous example. Later, carpets as floor coverings came

into vogue, along with painted floor cloths; both were advertised for sale in Williamsburg. Turkey, Wilton, and Scotch carpets were among other types used. Among the papers of John Norton & Sons, merchants of London and Virginia, is an invoice of August 14, 1769, listing, together with other articles to be sent "by the first Ship for York River," to Mrs. Martha Jacquelin "2 Kilmarnock [Scotch] Carpets, 1 large & 1 small [and] 1 painted duck Floor Cloth." Painted floor cloths were cheaper substitutes for carpets and may be considered the forerunners of our linoleum and oilcloth. They were made of stout canvas coated with oil paint and printed with a pattern, and were generally used on stairs and in halls and rooms of lesser importance. Rush mats were also in use throughout the century.

PAINTING AND THE USE OF COLOR

In eighteenth-century Virginia, the range of colors from which the painter could choose was restricted compared to the wide variety at his disposal today. Paints were purchased in England, and numerous invoices, letters, and advertisements have provided reasonably complete information as to paint ingredients available at the time. For example, William Allason, a wholesale merchant of Falmouth, Virginia, from 1760 to 1790, lists in his "invoice book" such inventories as:

> On hand—Copperas, 16 pounds
> Indigo
> Light Blue
> Chalk
> 10 Casks White Lead
> 1 Cask Red Lead
> 1 Cask Spanish Brown
> Red Paint from Maryland
> Linseed Oil, 10 gall.

These ingredients and certain others such as burnt umber, yellow ocher, orpiment, verdigris, litharge, Spanish whiting, lime for whitewash, archil, and walnut oil constituted the palette with which the colonial painter worked.

In those days painters used both oil and water paints. Linseed oil, made of ground flaxseed, and oil of walnut were the vehicles used in oil paints. Although both of these were produced in the colony, they were also frequently imported. Of the two, wal-

The speaker's chair in the House of Burgesses Chamber at the Capitol dates from about 1755.

nut oil was the first to be used, and it was considered better than linseed oil for interior work, "for Lindseed Oyl within doors will turn yellow, and spoil the beauty of it [the paint]; which . . . Walnut-Oyl . . . prevents; for that makes it keep a constant whiteness." Oil of turpentine, a rapid-drying spirit obtained from native yellow pine, was often used as a thinner.

White lead (carbonate of lead), called a body pigment because it forms the bulk of the paint, was, in colonial times as today, a primary ingredient of oil paints. There were two chief varieties, one called ceruse, which was the purest and cleanest sort, and the other simply white lead; a third, flake white, is spoken of as scarce and dear, "to be found only under the Lead [roofs] of some very old Buildings, where time has by the assistance of some sharp quality in the Air, thus reduced the undermost superficies of the Lead." The color pigments, reds, blues, greens, yellows, and browns, were derived from natural earths (Spanish brown, burnt umber, yellow ocher); from metals (copperas, verdigris, orpiment, and red lead); and from plants (indigo and archil).

Whitewash, a water paint, was made in the eighteenth century, as it is now, by slaking quicklime in water. The limewash was often colored in the nineteenth century by the addition of various pigments. Copperas (sulphate of iron), for example, was added to make it green; ocher, to give it a yellow hue; and archil, a color obtained from the liverwort plant, to produce a deep blue tone. Archil, once employed by the Romans, had been used in England since the Middle Ages to decorate the inside walls (and occasionally the outside stonework) of houses. Milk and buttermilk, furthermore, were occasionally used as vehicles in these color washes.

Walls and ceilings in eighteenth-century Virginia were commonly whitewashed once a year, although it might be done more often as a sanitary measure. The exteriors of frame buildings were likewise frequently whitewashed during the colonial period, as were brick structures late in the eighteenth century. In the case of brick buildings, the lime wash served more than a decorative function, since it formed a hard, crystalline coating on the brick and helped to preserve it. Whitewash continued in use throughout the century, as indicated by a notice of 1792 in the *Calendar of Virginia State Papers* "that Dabney Minor be directed to whitewash the Pedestals upon the top of the Capitol [in

Upstairs in the Capitol is the Virginia Council Chamber. The painting is of Queen Anne.

Richmond], & the Pilasters with Stone Lime, with a mixture of Lamp black to give it the resemblance of stone."

Of the oil colors used in exterior painting in Williamsburg during the eighteenth century, Spanish brown was a favorite. John Smith, philomath, an early authority on house painting, characterized it as "a dark, dull red, of a Horse-flesh colour, 'tis an Earth, it being dug out of the ground, but there is some of it of a colour pleasant enough to the Eye . . . 'tis of great use among Painters, being generally used as the first and primary colour, that they lay upon any kind of timber work, being cheap and plentiful." Spanish brown served on occasion as the finish coat both in interior and exterior work, and it is likely that many Williamsburg houses were of this color. Other colors much in vogue during the first half of the eighteenth century for exterior and interior woodwork were lead color, made of a mixture of indigo and white, and stone color, a white with a slight bluish tint. If the accounts of travelers of the time are to be accepted, however, white was the prevailing color for house exteriors in Williamsburg. Though fences were generally whitewashed or painted, evidence indicates that they were sometimes coated with pine tar as a protection against the weather. One writer of the time, in fact, states that "The common peoples houses . . . [in Virginia] are in general tarr'd all over to preserve them instead of Painting."

Interior woodwork was occasionally left in a natural state, but more often it was painted. Stone and wood colors, Spanish brown, and white were favorites for window frames and bars, doors, stair rails and balusters, mantels, paneling, cornices, and other trim. Greens were also used and, of these, verdigris, a green made of copper rust and inclining to bluish, was considered the best and most useful. This color, or one like it, was used to produce some of the familiar blue-green colors of Williamsburg. Shades of yellow and "timber" colors, colors used to imitate the tones of natural woods, vied with these in popularity. Frequent mention is made, for example, of "wainscot" color, umber mixed with white in imitation of oaken wainscot. Olive wood was simulated by ocher, mixed with a little white, veined over with burnt umber; walnut, by burnt umber and white, with veining of burnt umber and black. These last two imitations are early instances of graining. Other popular methods of finishing interior woodwork were: the painting of wainscoting, doors, and other trim to resemble marble—a treatment known to have been specified for the Council

Marbleized wood baseboard. Photograph of actual eighteenth-century example.

Chamber and other parts of the Capitol; painting to imitate tortoise shell; and staining. Skirting (baseboards) was customarily painted black in Virginia.

Much of the furniture of the eighteenth-century living room or parlor, that "fair lower room designed primarily for the entertainment of company," was comparable to that in our own houses. A spinet or harpsichord, for example, took the place of our piano, and a barrel organ (the record player of the day) might have been found. Despite the vehement objections of such strict moralists as the Reverend William Stith, who preached before the General Assembly in 1752 on "The Sinfulness and pernicious Nature of Gaming," a drop-leaf card table for piquet or dice often stood in readiness against one wall. The fireplace had its complement of "fire-dogs" (andirons), tongs, shovel, and bellows, a chimney board to close the fireplace opening when not in use, and possibly an adjustable embroidered screen to protect the face from the direct heat of the fire. Other furnishings might include a writing table equipped with a pewter inkwell, quill pens, and blotting sand; a snuffbox; a small locked cabinet for valuables; and a family Bible in its sturdy box, together with a few other books such as a copy of Warner's *Almanack, A Treatise on the Diseases of Virginia,* and *The Young Man's Best Companion.* Looking glasses were a favorite wall decoration; the living room would possibly have had a facing pair on opposite walls. Pictures were less numerous than today, but there might be a few engravings hung on the walls of the living room and other rooms, together possibly with a map of Virginia, a family portrait or two executed by some artist temporarily resident in Williamsburg, and, if the house were that of a wealthier person, a few paintings imported from England or Italy. Matthew Pratt, itinerant American "Portrait Painter, lately from England and Ireland, but last from New York," announced in the *Virginia Gazette* in 1773 that he had "brought with him to *Williamsburg* a small but very neat Collection of PAINTINGS, which are now exhibiting at Mrs. VOBE's near the Capitol; among which are . . . a very good Copy of *Corregio*'s ST. JEROME. . . . VENUS and CUPID, the only Copy from an original Picture by Mr. *West*. . . . A HOLY FAMILY. . . . A copy of *Guido's* JUPITER and EUROPA. . . . FLORA, a Companion to the above . . . [and] a very fine FRUIT PIECE."

The dining room in its furnishings was much the same as that of today. Food usually had to be carried to the house from an outside kitchen, however, and for this reason trivets, used in rewarming hot dishes, were kept at the fireplace. Other dining-room accessories often seen in the eighteenth century but rarely found today included pewter plates, sometimes with hot-water reservoirs to keep the food warm, napkin presses, knife boxes, tea caddies, spice chests in which the rarer luxuries were kept under lock and key, and horn tumblers, less expensive and more durable than glass. A corner cupboard might hold and display the fine ceramics, glass, pewter, and silver of the household, and a wine cellaret was indispensable.

Cooking was almost always done in buildings separate from the main house to reduce the fire hazard and to keep odors and excess heat from the house. The character of these kitchens was far different from those of today, because the food was cooked over an open flame in the great fireplace or in an oven actually built into the side of the chimney. Cooking over an open fire required cranes and spits, together with skillets and other cooking utensils with long handles. Kitchen equipment included many ingenious devices, such as automatic spits, toasters, reflector ovens, waffle irons, coffee grinders, roasters, and mixers, which were the forerunners of twentieth-century appliances. Utensils were of wood, pewter, brass, copper, and bell metal, as well as of iron and tin. Candle molds, butter churns, wine presses, and sausage machines were customary kitchen and service equipment. Houses often had an outside dairy, and a smokehouse for the curing of meat.

The bedchamber contained one or more four-poster canopied beds, with draw curtains to keep out draughts. A low trundle bed on casters occasionally stood beside the master bed and could be rolled under it when not in use. Bedding usually consisted of feather or flock mattresses, quilts, blankets, and sometimes hemp, canvas, or linen sheets. Closets, an innovation of the eighteenth century, were usually inadequate; large paneled wardrobes or presses, high boys, low boys, chest-on-chests, and trunks had to be provided.

Bed warmers, foot warmers, braziers, and other supplementary heating devices were found in all houses, and cast-iron backs were used in fireplaces to protect the brick from the heat. These fire backs, originally a utilitarian feature, became objects for decorative treatment and were ornamented with coats-of-arms, Biblical themes, and other subjects. The chief source of lighting was the candle, made both of the wax of the bayberry and of tallow. Chandeliers, sconces (with silver or mirror reflectors), candelabra, and individual candlesticks were provided to hold

The central passage and stairway of the Wythe House have the generous dimensions that characterized colonial Virginia architecture. With double doors at either end and plenty of width, the center passage became a breezy living area in the heat of summer.

them. Hurricane shades of glass were used to shield the candle flame from draughts.

Illumination was far from adequate by today's standards; the Palace, even when fully candle-lit for a splendid ball or banquet, would have appeared dimly

33

lighted to a twentieth-century spectator. Philip Fithian, writing in his journal of a sumptuous dinner at Nomini Hall, remarked that "The room looked luminous and splendid; four very large candles burning on the table where we supp'd, three others in different parts of the Room." Betty lamps and similar devices burning oil and fat were apparently seldom used in

Hurricane candle shade.

Virginia. A more primitive and cheaper source of light than candles was rushes dipped in scalding fat or grease. One ingenious practice of the time was to whitewash the cheeks and backs of fireplaces to reflect the light of the fire and aid in the illumination of the room. This was especially effective when pine knots, which produce a brilliant flame, were burned.

THE FURNISHING OF EXHIBITION BUILDINGS

In furnishing exhibition buildings, Colonial Williamsburg has been guided by documentary evidence as well as by close study of eighteenth-century furnishings and accessories. Inventories have been invaluable, especially at the Raleigh Tavern and the Palace. Public records, diaries, and correspondence have also revealed clues. Since original pieces specified in documents were rarely available, antiques similar to them were substituted, or, in exceptional cases, reproductions were authorized.

At the Capitol much of the required furniture was of such a type or was needed in such quantities that antique equivalents could not be obtained. Authentic reproductions were therefore made to represent the pieces originally in the building. Many antique pieces were also used, however, and the speaker's chair in the House of Burgesses is the very chair which stood in this hall in the eighteenth century. All of the paintings and books are antique.

The furnishings in the Palace are predominantly English, representing the various fashions found in the building during its existence. They are antique throughout except for two of the three magnificent crystal chandeliers in the ballroom, which had to be specially reproduced. The search for authentic pieces, which still continues, has often been prolonged and far-reaching. It is usually successful, however; for example, eleven Chelsea figures mentioned in an inventory entry have been placed in the dining room and ten of eleven have been found for the parlor.

In the house of George Wythe, a native Virginian, antiques of American origin predominate as contrasted with the English pieces found in the governor's home. No inventory of the Wythe House exists, so that those of comparable houses were followed. Styles of the late eighteenth century are here mingled with earlier pieces. Although no independent furniture forms were developed in Virginia and the pieces show a direct relationship to English prototypes, many of them have been modified by the colonial cabinetmakers.

RECIPE FOR COOKING VIRGINIA HAM

The following recipe is written on the flyleaf of a Bible that belonged to Colonel William Byrd of Westover.

To eat the Ham in Perfection steep it in Half Milk and half water for Thirty-six hours, and then having brought the Water to a Boil put the Ham therein and let it Simmer, not boil, for 4 or 5 Hours according to size of the Ham—for Simmering brings the Salt out and boiling drives it in.

The Gardens of Williamsburg

*God Almightie first planted a Garden. And indeed
it is the purest of humane pleasures. It is the greatest refreshment to the spirits of man; without
which Buildings and Palaces are but grosse handy-
works. . . .*

—Francis Bacon

Most of the original colonial gardens of Williamsburg had disappeared
before the effort began to re-create them. Portions of old walks,
fences, and some outbuildings remained. Remnants of boxwood hedges and
other evidences of eighteenth- and nineteenth-century gardens still existed.
These, along with listings of plant materials preserved in diaries, letters, and
the records of naturalists, served as a basis for re-establishing the gardens.

Those who kept gardens in eighteenth-century Williamsburg maintained
orderly plots. They considered the plan of the grounds and the various
features of the site—the outbuildings, gardens, and connecting walks—
bringing them into a regularized relationship with the house that was both
satisfying aesthetically and sound from the standpoint of use. The dependencies were never directly connected with the house in this region where
the winters were mild, and the warm, humid summers made ample circulation of air important. Typically, a kitchen, dairy, smokehouse, and well were
placed about an outside working area or service court paved with brick or
marl, at the side or rear of the main house. A stable and coach house with
an area for maintenance work and a paddock were generally located at the
back of the lot.

When the main house was situated on a street corner, a special type of
plan layout was occasionally developed. Here, since access to the property

could be gained from the side street, stables, store-houses, and other service buildings were placed along this street. Thus the house with its dependencies took the form of an L.

Between the various outbuildings or beside them were placed the kitchen and fruit gardens. Often they were combined into one planted area of vegetables, fruits, flowers, and medicinal herbs. Occasionally, in more elaborate gardens there may have been separate areas of ornamental planting set aside as a pleasure ground.

Joseph Prentis of Williamsburg kept a careful diary in the years 1784–88 of his gardening activities, from which comes this revealing excerpt of March 1784:

Sowed Early Pease in the[e] Square next Chimney. the 17th.
19. Sowed Rape Seed in the same Square.
Glory of England, sowed same Day in Square nex[t] Street oposite.
19. Sowed Carrots in this Squ[are]
19. Transplanted Rose Bus[hes] and Raspbarries
19. Sowed Lettuce seed.

Garden walks were usually of brick or marl, but other surfacing, such as gravel, oyster and scallop shells, and brickbats, was common. As a general rule, early designers were practical in their arrangement of service walks, which were laid to connect work areas in the most direct fashion, with few deviations for the sake of design. In the pleasure areas, however, where balance and form took precedence, the contrary was true.

Few indications of the existence of ornamental garden features have been found in studying records and archaeological remains. The Palace gardens, however, did make relatively extensive use of elaborate gates, decorative piers and termini, vases, steps, seats, garden houses, and enclosing walls. The smaller gardens achieved interest, for the most part, through the balance of outbuildings, walks, and fences. No evidence has been found of lead figures or fountains such as were used in English and Continental gardens.

Fences, so familiar in the Williamsburg scene today, were required by colonial law to be built around each lot. An act of the General Assembly of 1705, designed to protect the gardens from stray horses and cattle, required the owner of every half-acre lot contiguous to Duke of Gloucester Street to "inclose the said lots, or half acres, with a wall, pails, or post and rails, within

six months after the building, which the law requires to be erected thereupon, shall be finished." The height of the fence was set at four and one-half feet. Another act, applying to the colony in general, permitted the substitution for the fence of a so-called "quick-set" hedge. Such hedges, or "live fences," were made by digging a ditch and planting an impenetrable shrub on the top of the ridge of earth thrown up at the side.

Brick walls with molded brick copings were, in the town itself, usually confined to the enclosure of the grounds of public buildings. Post and rail fences and paling (picket fences) specified in the act became typical for private gardens, and fences of wattle (woven twigs) were also found. The "worm" or "snake" fence was frequently used to enclose fields in and about Williamsburg; this was a fence without posts made of six- or eight-foot rails laid zigzag fashion with ends interlocking—the familiar "Virginia rail" fence which continued in common use until replaced by wire fencing near the end of the nineteenth century.

The native persimmon, *Diospyros virginiana*, was often described in eighteenth-century English garden books as a desirable "exotic" from North America. Reproduced by permission from L. H. Bailey, *Standard Cyclopedia of Horticulture*.

PLANT MATERIALS

Of the trees and shrubs grown in the colonial gardens, some were imported at various times and others were native to Virginia. Holly hedges and trees were found in the gardens of Williamsburg; although some of this holly was brought from England, it was transplanted with difficulty and most of the old specimens are native. Records show that English yew was

A vegetable garden such as most Williamsburg homes might have had.
This one is behind the Pasteur-Galt Apothecary Shop.

brought to Virginia in the hope that it would make satisfactory hedges, but the colonists found the climate usually too dry to permit it to flourish. Both hawthorn and privet were imported. Boxwood and the native yaupon were also planted.

Among flowering shrubs which in recent years grew extensively in Williamsburg, forsythia has been removed from the Historic Area since it was found to have been introduced in the nineteenth century. The flowering quince ("japonica"), once removed for a like reason, is being reinstated; research established that it was introduced shortly before 1800.

Of the trees seen by the visitor, perhaps the most striking is the paper mulberry with its complex of gnarled trunks and its pulpy outer shell. It is a popular misconception that these trees were used in the colonial silkworm industry; the silkworm was actually reared on the true mulberry, the black and white. A number of true mulberry trees are to be found in Williamsburg, one of the finest being the ancient gnarled tree which overhangs the east wall of the Capitol.

Prominent among ornamental trees available to gardeners of the eighteenth century were the native species noted for the beauty of their flowers, such as the dogwood, *Magnolia grandiflora*, redbud, and catalpa. Trees that provided shade were the elm, sycamore, tulip, and pecan. The *Juniperus virginiana*, commonly called red cedar, was traditionally used as a

GENTLEMEN and others, may be supply'd with good Garden Peafe, Beans, and feveral other Sorts of Garden Seeds: Alfo, with great Choice of Flower Roots; likewife Trees of feveral Sorts and Sizes, fit to plant, as Ornaments in Gentlemen's Gardens, at very reafonable Rates, by Thomas Creafe, Gardener to the College, in Williamsburg.

border along either side of plantation approaches, and avenues of these may still be seen throughout Virginia.

Fruit trees were important in Williamsburg gardens. Governor Nicholson, in laying out the town in half-acre lots, specified that each person should have sufficient ground for his house, his garden, and orchard. Fruit had been useful to the settlers of Virginia from the outset. "Fruit growing in early colonial days," says S. W. Fletcher, in *A History of Fruit Growing in Virginia* (1932), "was chiefly for the purpose of securing a supply of 'most excellent and comfortable' drinks. . . . We have the word of Captain John Smith that 'few of the upper class planters drink any water.' " The first colonists found in abundance palatable small fruits such as grapes and berries: wild strawberries, huckleberries, blackberries, and raspberries. Of the tree fruits which the land afforded, the crab apple was small and bitter, the wild cherry practically worthless, the plums inferior in quality to European sorts, and, as for the persimmon, Captain Smith wrote "if it be not ripe it will draw a man's mouth awrie, with much torment." There were no native pears or peaches, and these, together with the apple, quince, plum, cherry, apricot, and nectarine were introduced from Europe. In the eighteenth century, fruit was frequently used in making liquors—wine, cider, perry (pear cider), peach brandy, and other fermented fruit juices.

Trees were of still more vital importance to Williamsburg and the colonies as the source of the raw materials for building, cabinetmaking, and the production of household utensils. Cedar, cypress, yellow pine, oak, elm, and beech were used in building, whereas walnut, the "cabinetmaker's wood," together with pine, cherry, applewood, and holly for inlay work, were employed in furniture manufacture. Farm implements were fashioned of wood (oak, ash, and hickory), often to the complete exclusion of any metal, leather, or fiber. Household manufacture of wooden ware achieved a high development as a craft. Poplar, ash, and alder were used to create objects of grace and endurance such as spoons, ladles, churns, buckets, trays, milk pails, and many other articles of domestic use.

In a day when chemical dyes were largely unknown, dyes for the coloring of cotton, linen, and wool were obtained directly from plant materials. The barks, roots, and leaves of trees as well as berries and flowers were sources of dye colors. Many varying shades of blue, for instance, were obtainable from the indigo plant, and the madder vine gave a wide range of shades from turkey-red to pink. Among the colors derived from barks were yellow and dark brown from the black walnut; golden brown from chestnut oak; green from hickory; black from willow; and gold from the black oak. The sumac berry yielded gray, and the petals of the poppy were a source of crimson. These were but a few of the many colors made from plant materials in the eighteenth century. Certain of these dyes were produced in quantity and exported from the colony, whereas others, such as a black made from logwood and a reddish brown from brazilwood, were derived from imported woods. Natural dyes are still made by native craftsmen in the highlands of southern Virginia and North Carolina and are considered by many superior to more commonly used chemical colors.

JOHN CUSTIS AND HIS GARDEN

A Williamsburg garden which no longer exists but which was, nevertheless, one of the best known in Virginia, was that of Colonel John Custis, father-in-law of Martha Dandridge Custis, who became the wife of George Washington. Custis, a councilor of the colony, built a house with a large garden in Williamsburg when he found that his home at Arlington on the Eastern Shore was too remote from the city. He was an eager student of the ways of nature and a lover of all growing things; he labored for twenty years in his garden, furnishing it with all manner of plants, trees, and shrubs, many native to the new country and some imported from England and elsewhere.

Custis apparently began his gardening venture in 1717, because in a letter of that year to his merchants in England he wrote: "I have lately got into the vein of gardening and have made a handsome garden to my house; and desire you will lay out 45 [£] for me in handsome striped hollys and yew but most hollys." A large proportion of his plant materials succumbed on

"Quick-set" hedge, an enclosure made by digging a ditch and planting the mound thus produced with a quick-growing hedge.

the way to Williamsburg, and in later letters he complains bitterly about the lack of care used in their packing and the stupidity of ship captains who allowed them to die on the way: "The box for my garden was all rotten as dirt did not save one sprig; the gardener was either a fool or a knave and by his management never packed anything before to go beyond sea."

Sir John Randolph of Williamsburg was instrumental in bringing Custis in touch with Peter Collinson of London, a wool draper whose hobby was gardening and whom years of experiment had made an expert botanist and naturalist. Collinson was deeply interested in the flora and fauna of the colonies and had become acquainted with several Americans, including William Byrd of Westover, who sent him plants and seeds from their gardens. A few extracts from letters written by Custis to Collinson in 1735 give an idea of the plants exchanged and a glimpse into the Custis garden: "I have planted the Pistacious Nutts and I think I shall allmonds. I have allmond trees that thrive well, but they bloom so early that it is not once in a great many years but the frost kills the blossoms. . . . I have planted the dates, but I doubt they are too tender to do well here. I have planted the seeds of the Cedar of Lebanon. . . . As for those peas you call Italian beans we call them black eyed Indian peas, and I make yearly hundreds of bushels of them and ship them to the West Indies."

Among Collinson's American friends was John Bartram of Pennsylvania, a farmer who became one of the country's greatest naturalists and whose garden on the Schuylkill near Philadelphia was one of America's first botanical gardens. Acting at the suggestion of Collin-

son, Bartram toured Maryland and Virginia, stopping off in Williamsburg to make the acquaintance of John Custis. Custis later wrote Collinson of the visit of the famous naturalist: "He [Mr. Bartram] is the most taking facetious man I ever met with and [I] never was so delighted with a stranger in all my life. I have had a letter from him . . . with his kind offers to send me some Dutch white currant bushes which would be very acceptable."

Thus Custis became acquainted with Bartram, and a triangular correspondence among three of the most active naturalists of the day was begun. Two, Collinson and Bartram, created gardens filled with the curiosities yielded by eighteenth-century plant exploration. Of the Custis garden nothing remains which can with certainty be said to have been planted by his hand. However, near the Custis Kitchen, the only one of his buildings which still exists, there stands an old yew tree which may well be a descendant of those which he planted and tended with so much care.

THE RE-CREATION OF THE GARDENS

Plant materials other than trees, bulbs, and a few shrubs do not survive a century unless carefully tended. When trees and hedges do last, as in the case of the old boxwood of the Brush-Everard garden, they have proved a valuable aid in determining the early design pattern of the garden.

There was a variety of fence and gate posts in Williamsburg.

Archaeological studies, in the course of which known sites of old gardens were excavated and examined, have been of great assistance in restoration work. Features of the original landscape plan, such as remains of outbuilding foundations, brick and marl walks, paved service areas, surface drains, and old wall and fencepost lines, as well as plant material preserved in abandoned well shafts, have been found. In many cases, walks uncovered several inches below the surface revealed a garden axis, possible size and shape of planting areas, and the general lot layout.

Additional information on the arrangement of gardens and outbuildings was found through research into old records such as insurance policies, which frequently included sketches of the lots; descriptions in travel accounts and old letters; eighteenth-century maps of the town such as the Frenchman's Map; and nineteenth-century photographs. Finally, study of surviving remains of gardens in the surrounding tidewater region and of the Sauthier plans of North Carolina towns of the eighteenth century has been of great assistance in determining approximate plantings as well as the general character of garden designs.

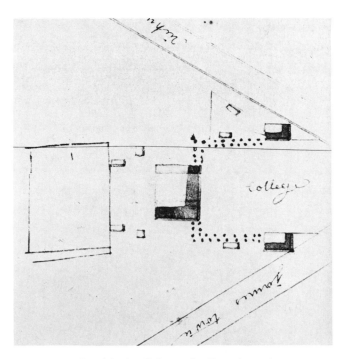

On this detail from the Frenchman's Map, the double lines of dots framing the college yard are presumed to indicate tree-bordered walks.

EXAMPLES OF GARDEN LAYOUTS

The Wythe Garden

The site plan of the George Wythe House and outbuildings is an example of an L-shaped scheme. Service structures and their surrounding yards have been placed along the side street. Following traces revealed by excavation, a main axial walk with parallel side paths and a lawn terminating in a low mound and arbor have been developed at the rear of the house. Balancing small outbuildings accent the farther corners of the mall, much as the north garden of the Palace is terminated by necessary houses (the eighteenth-century privy).

Fruit and kitchen gardens along one side of the central mall balance the service areas along the other. Vegetable and fruit-tree plantings are interwoven, and fig bushes have been used along one side of the garden. A small herb plot south of the main house shows the use of medicinal and culinary herbs.

The Bryan Garden

The Bryan House layout is typical of plans in which the pleasure garden is located at the side of the house. The plan follows the usual colonial pattern, with the kitchen, smokehouse, and service area located at the rear of the house and the stable yard with its paddock at the back of the lot. The intervening space between kitchen area and stable yard has been developed as a small kitchen garden, whose four plots would be of sufficient size to supply "sallots," herbs, and vegetables.

The pleasure garden has been patterned after examples illustrated in the Sauthier maps, in which a square or circular central design is often shown. In the Bryan garden, central and axial layouts have been combined, but from the street this garden appears axial, featuring a live oak, arch, and seat at the south. Along its minor cross axis the garden appears as a central type, with its square center and four topiary pieces the most conspicuous objects.

The Palace Gardens

The Palace layout is as formal and elaborate as the furnishings and architecture of the Palace itself; this was an early example of the formal garden in Virginia,

This view of the formal garden behind the Governor's Palace emphasizes the geometrical character of the most elaborate of Williamsburg's gardens.

being preceded and rivaled in extent only by Governor Berkeley's garden at Green Spring.

The forecourt design, with its four oval planting beds, stone walks, narrow entrance gate, and curved enclosing walls, is derived from the engraver's delineation on the Bodleian Plate, an eighteenth-century copperplate discovered in the Bodleian Library at Oxford. The service yard, to the west of the west flanking building, contains the buildings necessary for the maintenance of a large household—kitchen, scullery, salt and meat houses, smokehouse, laundry, and related outbuildings. This noisy, active area was placed as far away from the governor's living apartments as demands of service would permit.

The boundaries of the ballroom garden were discovered by excavation of long-hidden wall foundations. The main building axis and foundations of the north gate set the line for the broad central walk. The position of the main cross walk, likewise, was fixed by the east and west gate foundations. The detail design of the diamond-shaped parterres (ornamental arrangements of beds or plots) was adapted from those shown on the Bodleian Plate. The lead vases were listed in Palace inventories.

The north garden continues at a slightly lower level on either side of the main central axis and reflects familiar forms used in late seventeenth-century England: topiary, pleached arbors, and tulip plantings. The architectural enclosure of brick walls with interspersed piers, the elegant iron-work of gates, grilles, and clairvoyees, the steps and decorative piers with lead vases, and the corner necessary houses, are all fundamental component features of this design mode.

At the east of the ballroom garden is the plain parterre or tree-box garden, and at the west a box garden laid out in a quadrangle of squares and circles. This adjoins the Revolutionary burying ground, in which the bodies of 156 soldiers were found.

To the north of the burying ground is a fruit garden enclosed by a brick wall, against which figs are espaliered. Nectarines are trained on wooden supports and the exotic pomegranate grows in the fruit garden. Behind the garden are the holly maze, patterned after that at Hampton Court, England, and the mount, a terraced mound of earth in the shape of a truncated pyramid, with a flight of steps leading to a platform at the top. Both the maze and the mount are also late seventeenth-century landscape features.

The Restoration of an American Town

*"He who alters an old House is ty'd as a Translator
to the Original, and is confin'd to the Fancy of the
first Builder. Such a Man would be unwise to pull
down a good old Building, perhaps to erect a worse
new one."*

—*Builder's Dictionary, 1734*

THE RESTORATION of Williamsburg represents the
first attempt on a large scale to recover the physical form and atmosphere of an entire colonial town. It
has been undertaken with the conviction that our old
buildings with their furniture and implements are the
visual memorials of our early history—"the scene and
witness of human adventures and events." The realization that a wealth of historic fact and artistic value
lay hidden in the venerable remains of Williamsburg
led to its restoration.

Only recently has America come to recognize the
cultural values in its past architecture, although historic buildings have always had their loyal protectors.
Mount Vernon, Independence Hall, and the Old State
House at Boston were early accepted as historic
monuments, as well as many other significant buildings in all sections of the country. Inexperience or
misdirected enthusiasm sometimes led to faulty restoration work which caused even more damage to a
building than indifference or neglect; but gradually
there has grown up a tradition of preserving the original expression as well as the actual physical structure
of buildings.

What has come to be called the restoration of ancient buildings owes something to the architect
Thomas Ustick Walter, designer of the great dome of
the national Capitol. Walter, who was perhaps America's first "restorer," was asked by a building committee to make changes to the interior of old Christ
Church in Philadelphia, in the year 1834. Before ac-
cepting the commission, Walter remarked to the sponsors: "I have often looked with regret at the innovations on the purity of the architecture of Christ
Church. The propriety of reducing the height of the
ceiling and making it a flat surface has now been suggested. This would make the house easier to speak in,
and it could be warmed with more facility; but this
alteration would completely ruin the architecture of
the building, and destroy all that dignity and ecclesiastical effect so completely attained in this venerable
fabric."

It was at almost this same time—in 1838—that Bruton Parish Church in Williamsburg was considerably
"renovated," and not with the whole-hearted approval
of all parishioners. Miss Elizabeth Galt of Williamsburg, who was visiting in Brooklyn at the time, wrote
Dr. A. D. Galt in 1840 to inquire, "And do tell me, who
have been the Goths and the Vandals who have modernized our dear abbey?"

Since then, many organizations have been formed
for the care of historic buildings and to arouse public
interest in their behalf. Many of these are local or
regional in character. The Mount Vernon Ladies' Association, founded in 1853, is an early example. This
association acquired Mount Vernon in 1858 from
John Augustine Washington, Jr., who had tried without success to interest the United States government
in purchasing it as a national monument. In Virginia,
the Association for the Preservation of Virginia An-

tiquities has joined with state and local groups to protect historic sites. At Williamsburg, this society kept secure the foundations of the colonial Capitol, deeding them to its restorers when reconstruction was begun. The APVA, which has worked closely with the Williamsburg project from the start, also owns the site of the Magazine, which is now leased to Colonial Williamsburg.

Other societies worked on a national scale. The American Scenic and Historic Preservation Society was organized in 1895 and has pioneered in stimulating interest in America's architectural past. Another example is the Committee on Preservation of Historic Monuments of the American Institute of Architects, established in 1909. One of the most recent organizations formed on this nationwide basis is the National Trust for Historic Preservation, chartered by act of Congress in 1949. Supported entirely by the contributions of member organizations and individuals, it serves both as a clearinghouse of information and an advisor on problems of historic preservation. The federal government, in the Historic Sites Act of 1935, declared it "a national policy to preserve for public use historic sites, buildings and objects of national significance for the inspiration and benefit of the people of the United States." A year earlier, in 1934, the National Park Service initiated a major project with the establishment of a Historic American Buildings Survey to record, photograph, and make measured drawings of historic structures. This, and a companion study also dating from the thirties—the National Survey of Historic Sites and Buildings—were resumed with new vigor under the broad Mission 66 program of the National Park Service. The purpose has not been to acquire these places, but to point out the desirability of preserving them.

Throughout America, attempts to restore or preserve significant buildings and historic sites have become more frequent in recent years. Two of the best-known restoration projects were carried out in Virginia at Monticello and Stratford. Both are contemporary with the restoration of Colonial Williamsburg. Monticello was purchased by the Thomas Jefferson Foundation in 1929 and restored soon afterward. Stratford Hall, in Westmoreland County, Virginia, home of Robert E. Lee, was a larger undertaking. This property was conveyed to the Robert E. Lee Memorial Foundation in July 1929. It was restored under the

Early drawings of Williamsburg, early maps, inventories, land grants, newspaper advertisements, records of loss by fire, early insurance policies, all were considered in the process of restoration. The engraving above was made at some time before 1875.

direction of Fiske Kimball, architect, in 1932–35. The work done included the repair and preservation of the mansion and its dependencies. The gardens and orchards were also restored.

THE RESTORATION OF WILLIAMSBURG

The recovery of colonial Williamsburg was undertaken in fulfillment of a plan proposed to the late Mr. John D. Rockefeller, Jr., by Dr. W. A. R. Goodwin, late rector of Bruton Parish. The plan, almost prohibitively ambitious, was made possible only by vast expenditures and the continuing lively interest of the donor. The first steps in acquiring houses and lots and in developing the initial organization were taken in 1926.

The purpose of Colonial Williamsburg at the outset was to recover the significant portions of a historic and important city of America's colonial period. This purpose, always flexible in nature, has come to have a much broader significance. Not only are the buildings the subject for study, but also the life and thought associated with them. A new emphasis is placed upon the significance of the painstaking craftsman. In addition, a program of interpretation has been developed, based on the recognition of Williamsburg's importance in the formulation of American political thought, in education, commerce, fashions of the New World, and as a seat of religion.

The program, as it has been carried out, involved more than the repair and restoration of the many existing colonial homes and buildings. Other buildings, including the immensely significant Capitol and Palace, had disappeared, and had to be completely reconstructed on their original foundations. Authentic furnishings and decorations were required. Gardens had to be replanted.

To accomplish this, it was necessary to purchase or control virtually all the area that formerly comprised the colonial city. A vast staff of experts was employed: architects, archaeologists, landscape gardeners, builders, town planners, historians, lawyers, engineers, and many others. The architectural firm of Perry, Shaw and Hepburn was retained in 1927 to have direct charge of the architectural development and the manner of restoration. Their valued services continued until 1934 when a local architectural staff was formed at Williamsburg to carry to completion the original

restoration program and to maintain the buildings already erected and their gardens.

For the first two years the chief problem was that of research. Archives in America and Europe were searched for any record or reference that would aid

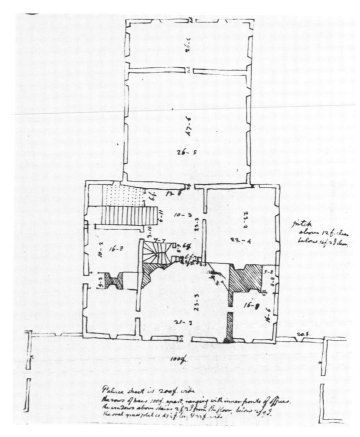

Measured drawing of the Palace, made by Thomas Jefferson, probably in 1779. This drawing was of great value to the architects in developing an authentic plan arrangement and in rebuilding the Palace.

the restoration work to follow. Supplementary archaeological evidence was sought. During this research stage, a number of extraordinary discoveries were made. In the Bodleian Library at Oxford, for example, an eighteenth-century copperplate was found on which were shown, as carefully engraved illustrations, the first Capitol at Williamsburg, the Governor's Palace, and the buildings of the College of William and Mary. This engraved plate was of great assistance to the architects in composing their designs, and is now on exhibition in Williamsburg. Two drawings by Thomas Jefferson were added to the pool of reference

45

The Governor's Palace, advance buildings, and parterres as they appeared about 1740 on the Bodleian Plate (see page 45).

Wood engraving of the Apollo Room at the Raleigh Tavern, made in 1848. This engraving indicated an early architectural treatment of the room.

The Prentis Store was stripped of its additions and restored.

RESTORATION

This photograph shows the John Crump House before the turn of the century. Built in stages during the 1700s, the house had as many as three tenants at one time.

A water-color drawing of the Greenhow-Repiton House. The house, demolished several decades ago, was reconstructed with the aid of this drawing.

An old photograph of the Scrivener House gave a clear picture of its early architectural appearance.

material. One, a ground-floor plan of the Palace made while Governor Jefferson lived there, is preserved among his papers at the Massachusetts Historical Society; it corroborated the archaeological evidence for reconstruction of the building. The second, located at the Huntington Library in California, was a carefully drawn proposal for the extension of the Wren Building at the College of William and Mary. Some years previously, a minutely detailed map of Williamsburg, probably drawn in 1782 and attributed to an anonymous French engineer, had been found in an antique

men in the employ of the architects. To co-ordinate and interpret the architectural and historical material, a separate Department of Research and Record was formed. When the scope of work began to include building interiors and furnishings, the assistance of specialists in those fields was called upon.

During the first full work year (1928), a committee of advisory architects, consisting of eight men with special competence in colonial architecture, was appointed. Although advisory in nature, this group passed on all plans and designs, as well as on the use

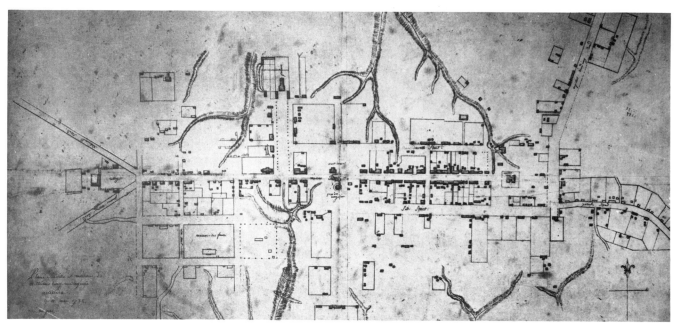

The Frenchman's Map is so called because it is believed to have been made by a French army mapmaker in 1782. It shows with accuracy the plan of the town and location of buildings and property lines just after the Revolution.

shop at Norfolk and presented to the college. This map, which came to be known as the "Frenchman's Map," proved an invaluable aid, since it shows the position of buildings of the town during the Revolutionary period. Additional military maps and surveys, prepared by French, English, and other army officers during their sojourn in Williamsburg at the time of the Revolution, were helpful.

The supervising architects at first were fully occupied with the design of buildings to be reconstructed and restored and in making measured drawings and photographs of plantation houses and gardens of the surrounding Virginia area. Much of the field work was prompted by the enthusiasm of drafts-

of precedent. In the course of their periodic meetings, a code of restoration principles and procedure was compiled which has served the architects as a guide:

1. All buildings or parts of buildings in which the colonial tradition persists should be retained irrespective of their actual date.

2. Where the classical tradition persists in buildings or parts of buildings, great discretion should be exercised before destroying them.

3. Within the "restoration area" all work which no longer represents colonial or classical tradition should be demolished or removed.

4. Old buildings in Williamsburg outside the "restoration area" wherever possible should be left and if possible pre-

served on their original sites and restored there rather than moved within the "area."

5. No surviving old work should be rebuilt for structural reasons if any reasonable additional trouble and expense would suffice to preserve it.

6. There should be held in the minds of the architects in the treatment of buildings the distinction between *Preservation* where the object is scrupulous retention of the surviving work by ordinary repair, and *Restoration* where the object is the recovery of the old form by new work; the largest practicable number of buildings should be preserved rather than restored.

7. Such preservation and restoration work requires a slower pace than ordinary modern construction work, and a superior result should be preferred to more rapid progress.

8. In restoration the use of old materials and details of the period and character, properly recorded, is commendable when they can be secured.

9. In the securing of old materials there should be no demolition or removal of buildings where there seems a reasonable prospect that they will persist intact on their original sites.

10. Where new materials must be used, they should be of a character approximating the old as closely as possible, but no attempt should be made to "antique" them by theatrical means.

To put these procedures into practice was often difficult. It is hard to tamper with an old building without destroying the attraction acquired by age. At the same time it is an accepted principle that parts must be repaired and known original details should be restored, such as in window sills and moldings, where sufficient fragments still exist. Repairs and cleaning-

Drawing of the Capitol on Bodleian Plate.

up add to the worth of an old building when these are done in a workmanlike manner that is obviously protective. "The best repair," according to Philip Webb, founder of England's Society for the Preservation of Ancient Buildings, "is a sort of building surgery which aims at conservation."

STEPS IN RESTORATION

In Williamsburg the restoration of a building is undertaken according to well-established procedure. The house to be restored is first examined under the direction of architects and draftsmen familiar with colonial building construction and design. To prepare the house for this preliminary study, the building is cleared of all vines; near-by shrubbery is removed. In some cases, trees must also be relocated. Grass around the foundation is cut back and convenient access made to all walls. Where necessary, walls in danger of collapse are shored up; inside floors are given support. Debris is removed from the house and all floors made "broom clean."

Measurements are then made of the interior and exterior of the house, including floor heights from basement to roof, and the relationship of floor heights to the outside grade. Sketches with measurements are drawn of walls, brickwork, floors, partitions, ornamentation, stairs, mantels, and windows and doors along with their framing. Wall surfaces are examined and special attention is given any evidence of changes or relathing. Color samples are obtained from the layers of paint. In the study of the foundation a record is kept of any deterioration, rotted sills, closed windows, and parts added or removed. Photographs, now including motion pictures, are periodically made of the restoration process to serve as a field record.

On most sites, archaeological excavations are carried out in a search for further evidence of the nature of a structure and its evolution. The excavators also expect to uncover the foundations of vanished outbuildings, expose post holes from lost fencelines, and trace the course of forgotten ditches and walkways. At the same time they invariably encounter a multitude of artifacts whose scholarly interpretation can throw new light on many aspects of Williamsburg's colonial life. Thus the archaeologists are able to assist museum personnel in the authentic re-creation of eighteenth-century crafts, help landscape architects select appropriate plant materials for the gardens, and, most im-

EXCAVATED FOUNDATION OF
THE GOVERNOR'S PALACE

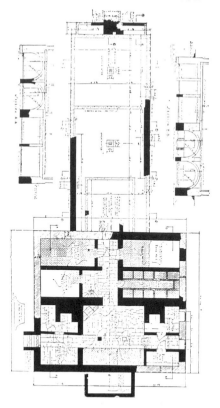

The Palace floor plan was revealed by painstaking excavation at the site. The completeness of the plan is shown by the drawing and photograph at the left, with original existing walls indicated in solid black in the drawing. The photograph above shows paving both of Purbeck stone and of brick.

portant, aid curators by providing precedents for items used in the furnishing of exhibition buildings.

Sometimes it is necessary to strip a part of the facing of the house down to the framing, in order to observe changes and examine its physical condition. This process of stripping has always been done with great caution and only where imperative. Old flooring and original window frames, even when partly rotted, are left alone. Rather than undertake a drastic replacement of the whole, repairs are made on whatever parts are splintered or decayed. Weatherboarding in bad condition is extremely difficult to put in a state of sound repair. In some instances the existing weatherboard-

ing, even though recent, is preferred to the complete smoothness of new siding.

When first-hand scrutiny of the house is completed, scale drawings of the structure are made. Modern additions are removed. An authentic sash replaces the modern sash found in place. The original cornice is restored, perhaps by following the profile of parts concealed beneath an added porch. Foundations are underpinned, and sills and window framings repaired.

In the meantime, research assistants have painstakingly gathered existing data on the history of the house, its owners or tenants, its use, and possibly even its appearance and the materials of which it was constructed. This information is derived from county records, town maps, abstracts of title, wills, inventories, and even advertisements from the local *Virginia Gazette.*

After this preliminary research and investigation is completed, work is begun. Of course, all of the missing evidence is rarely discovered: the age of a building or its additions is elusive, and the problem of replacing missing parts is often difficult.

The techniques for preserving, restoring, or reconstructing the buildings of Colonial Williamsburg have been developed through experience. New techniques are constantly being evolved. But the methods used for this work are always subordinate to the spirit of the whole undertaking—an attempt to recapture with authenticity the environment as well as the physical form of a small American town of two centuries ago.

A Photographic Tour of Williamsburg

These variously shaped roofs are those of the dependencies grouped about the service court of the Palace.

The illustrations that follow serve as preparation for seeing the town, as a helpful accompaniment to a walking tour, and as an accurate record of what has been seen in Williamsburg.

THE GOVERNOR'S PALACE

One approaches the Governor's Palace from Duke of Gloucester Street by way of a stately avenue bordered by catalpa trees. During the times of the royal governors, displays of fireworks were on occasion held here and in 1776 it was used as a parade ground.

The governor's house, ironically called the "Palace" because of the funds lavished upon its construction, was "a magnificent Structure, built at publick Expence, finished and beautified with Gates, fine Gardens, Offices, Walks, a fine Canal, Orchards, &c . . . by the ingenious Contrivance of the most accomplished Colonel Spotswood."

The Palace in colonial days was the scene of splendid social gatherings. At the yearly celebrations of the king's birthday, for example, it is said to have presented an appearance equalled and surpassed only by the Court of England. Inventories of the governors give ample evidence of the elaborateness of the Palace furnishings. In addition to furniture provided by the colony, the "standing furniture" of the Palace, each governor brought a large collection of his own. The Palace furniture ranged in character from the "newest fashion" of Governors Botetourt and Dunmore, to some items characterized by observers as "old fashion'd."

At right, the supper room, showing Chinese influence. *Below left*, English chandelier of same room. *Below right*, puzzle, "The Kings and Queens of England."

Right, the little dining room, used by the governor and his family. About the mahogany Chippendale table is a particularly fine set of Queen Anne chairs with original needlework seats. The tea set on the mantel is Whieldon agateware, and the bowl on the table is Lambeth delftware.

Below right, detail of mantel of little dining room, and *left,* detail of mantel in the bed-chamber over the parlor.

Opposite, the royal crown of England and the cypher of Queen Anne, both in gilded wrought-iron, grace the front gateway to the Governor's Palace. A stone unicorn crouches atop one of the gateposts, its partner, a stone lion, sits on the other.

The Brush-Everard House, a stone's throw from the Governor's Palace, is almost as old as the town itself. John Brush, first keeper of the Powder Magazine, purchased the lot in 1717 and finished building the original house while the Palace was being completed. The house was probably expanded about mid-century by Thomas Everard, clerk of York County. Though not wealthy, Everard was a man of comfortable, middle-class circumstances. As the furnishings of the parlor indicate, the restoration reflects his period of ownership.

56

THE GEORGE WYTHE HOUSE

George Wythe, an eminent lawyer who became the first professor of law in an American college, was also a signer of the Declaration of Independence. The youthful Jefferson frequently sat at his table, along with other students of the college, and learned lessons in the rights of man.

The house was large for Williamsburg but strikingly austere in its balanced architecture. Its design is credited to Richard Taliaferro, Wythe's father-in-law. The house plan is the "center hall" type, two rooms deep. Its gardens and outbuildings are arranged similarly to those of a small plantation.

57

The southeast bedroom of the Wythe House. The cherry chest-on-chest was made in New England in the mid-eighteenth century. The window and bed hangings are cotton resist dyed in two shades of blue. The table, *right*, is a forerunner of the modern dressing table. Gentlemen's wigs were placed on wig stands and powdered.

The student's room of the Wythe House. The mahogany table holds a terrestrial globe that might have been used by students in the eighteenth century. The microscope, *left*, made in London about 1725–30, stands in front of its case.

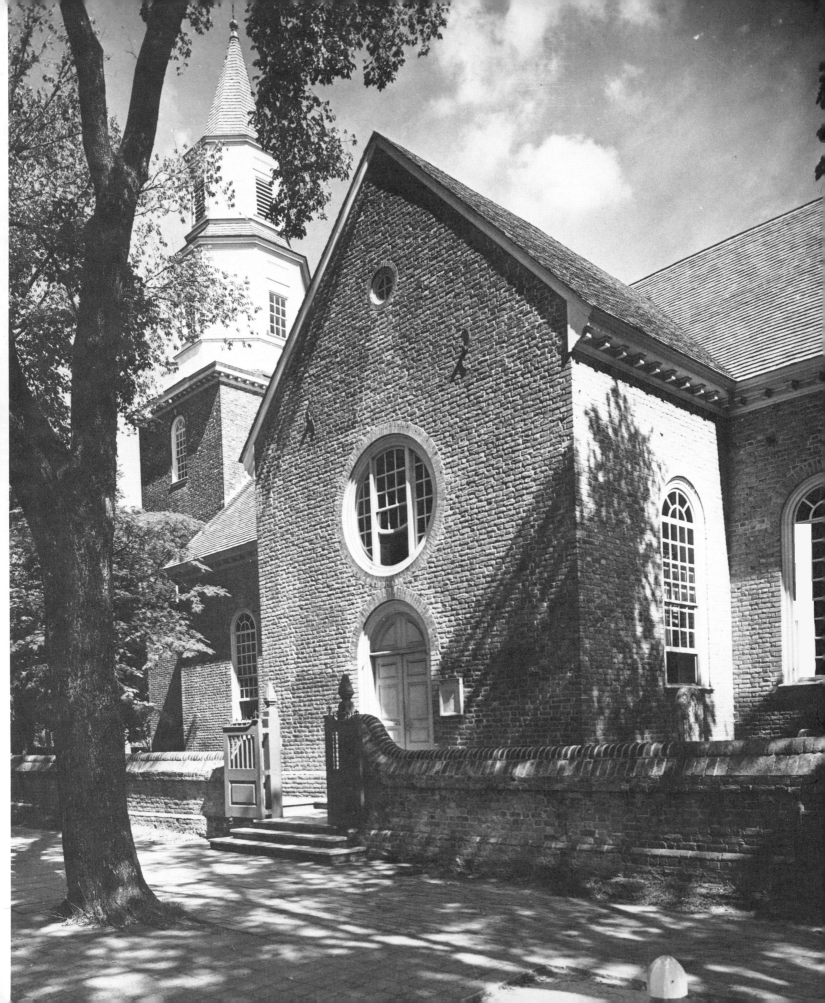

THE JAMES GEDDY HOUSE
AND SILVERSMITH SHOP

The Geddy house was erected about 1750, partly on foundations of an earlier structure owned and occupied by James Geddy, Sr., gunsmith. Its low-pitched roof without dormers makes it an architectural rarity in Williamsburg.

The younger James Geddy, silversmith, lived and worked here through the middle years of the eighteenth century. He and his brothers, who were brass founders, cutlers, and blacksmiths, helped greatly in the twentieth-century re-creation of their workshops by leaving around the premises a veritable treasure of debris—and some silver spoons—to be unearthed by today's archaeologists.

Opposite page, Bruton Parish Church

Right, a graceful brass wall sconce reproduced at the Geddy foundry, and below it the arm of the antique original used as pattern in one half of a sand casting mold.

The Magazine was built in 1715 to protect the arms, gunpowder, and ammunition of the colony. Lord Dunmore's secret removal of the powder caused the first assembling of an armed force in Virginia for what was to become the American Revolution.

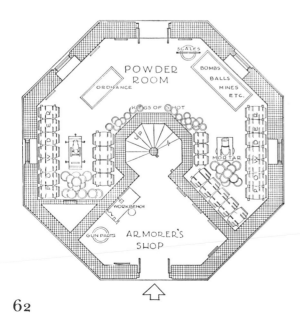

Mortars and gunpowder in barrels were stored on the ground floor of the Magazine, *left*, while racks above held pole arms, muskets, and the like. To protect the Magazine, which was considered "much exposed," a high brick wall was built around it and, near by, a Guardhouse.

The Courthouse on Market Square, erected in 1770. Four Doric columns, added to the portico after a fire in 1911, were omitted in the restoration of the building in 1932.

Courthouse during the 1870s.

Courthouse as restored after fire.

The corner of the Raleigh taproom is typical of an eighteenth-century bar.

RALEIGH TAVERN

At this tavern the leading patriots of Virginia gathered, before the Revolution and afterward, including George Washington, Patrick Henry, Thomas Jefferson, George Wythe, Peyton Randolph, George Mason.

Termed "the second capitol of the colony" because lawmakers convened here on several occasions after the Assembly was dissolved by an irate governor, in 1769 it was the scene for discussion and formulation of the nonimportation agreement. In 1774, an influential group of patriots met at the Raleigh to issue the call for the First Continental Congress.

WETHERBURN'S TAVERN

Henry Wetherburn, who for a time was host at the Raleigh Tavern, moved across the street and opened a rival hostelry in the earliest part of this building (to the left of the tree) about 1740. He added the extension to the right about ten years later, and the structure has been in continuous use ever since.

The room-by-room inventory made at the time of Wetherburn's death served as a principal guide in furnishing the restored tavern with antique articles similar to those listed. The inventory indicated that the tavernkeeper could make a total of nineteen beds available in rooms upstairs and down.

The Capitol was one of the principal buildings of colonial America. Of two capitol buildings that stood successively on this same site, the first (built 1701–05) was selected for reconstruction. At *right,* Conference Room.

General Court of the Capitol, *above*. This paneled room was set apart for the use of the General Court; across the hall was the office of the secretary of the colony.

Less imposing in architecture was the House of Burgesses, said to be similar in its appearance to the House of Commons of the mother country. The House of Burgesses, the Council, and the General Court of the Virginia colony met at the Capitol from 1704 to 1776.

The Capitol, looking upward toward the cupola, where once more flies the Great Union flag of England and Scotland in the eighteenth century.

Not far from the Capitol was built a Public Gaol, described as "a strong sweet Prison." Stocks and pillory once stood in the Capitol yard.

Opposite page, a common cell and leg irons.

At mid-century, Williamsburg was spoken of as offering an "agreeable residence." Most of the houses were of modest size, commonly a story and a half in height, with steep gabled roofs. These dwellings were generally framed with wood, "cased with feather-edged Plank, painted with white Lead and Oil, covered with Shingles." The illustration is of the Greenhow-Repiton House.

The Mary Stith Shop, one of the many modest buildings on shaded Duke of Gloucester Street, now contains an itinerant musician's room.

A SELECTION OF SMALL HOUSES

The gambrel roof became extremely popular in Williamsburg. Here are shown the William Lightfoot House, *at left;* the Tayloe House, *below left,* and, *below right,* the Orrell House. These houses are similar in their common possession of a side hallway, corner fireplaces with chimneys contained within the outside walls, and construction of wood frame, faced with weatherboards.

Opposite page. The upper illustration shows the Waters-Coleman House, with an exceptionally fine pair of brick chimneys. Sloped-roof closets of brick occur at each end of the front. This, and the Moody House, *lower left,* and the Travis House, *lower right,* have long sloping roofs at rear.

The Orlando Jones House, *above*, with its kitchen at the right, viewed from the garden side. The covered porch entry and chamber above are features found in early Virginia houses, notably Bacon's Castle.

The John Blair House, *left*, was at the time of the Revolution the home of John Blair, Jr. He later served as a Virginia delegate to the Constitutional Convention and a justice of the Supreme Court of the United States. The plan of the house originally consisted of a center hallway and entrance with a room on either side. It was later lengthened and a second doorway added.

The illustration on the *opposite page* shows the western doorway of the John Blair House with stone steps said to have come from the first theatre in Williamsburg.

This small shop may once have been devoted to the manufacture and sale of household articles made of tin. The unusual roof overhang, running the length of the building, serves as both a sun shade and a rain shelter.

Lightfoot House. Surrounding the house, at one time, were extensive gardens including "beautiful crape myrtles and pomegranate bushes."

St. George Tucker House, one of the few large houses of the town. Soon after the Revolution it became the home of St. George Tucker, second professor of law at the College of William and Mary.

79

The Semple House has a unique two-story center pavilion and balanced wings.

The older part of the Coke-Garrett House was erected before the Revolution. The goldsmith, John Coke, lived in it at one time. Its fine west staircase, *above*, is in what was popularly known as the Chinese Chippendale manner.

A shop, with separate entrances, was at one end of the James Anderson House. It adjoined the two-story main house, *right*.

The Brick House Tavern was reconstructed on old foundations. York County land records were of assistance in determining the floor arrangement.

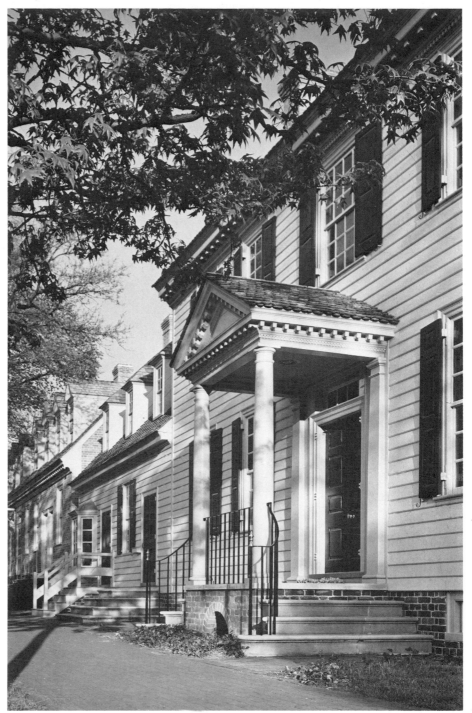

The James Anderson House is most notable for its associations with George Washington, a frequent visitor to Williamsburg. On November 5, 1768, he wrote in his diary, "Dined at Mrs. Campbell's, where I had spent all my Evenings since I came to Town." Mrs. Christiana Campbell kept this house as a tavern for a short time. The house, reconstructed, now contains an archaeological exhibit.

81

The Deane House, *above*, situated on the Palace Green, was for a while the home of Elkanah Deane, coachmaker, formerly of Dublin.

The Robert Carter House, *left*, was the town house of Robert Carter of Nomini Hall. It was given special prominence by its location next door to the Palace and for a brief period served as the house of the royal governor.

The Peyton Randolph House, of distinguished architectural simplicity, was at one time the home of Peyton Randolph, first president of the Continental Congress; it has been identified as the headquarters of General Rochambeau in 1781; General Lafayette was entertained here on the occasion of his visit to Williamsburg in 1824.

Josiah Chowning's Tavern, built on the site of an early inn.

1

Kitchens were placed away from the house as a protection from the heat of cookery. Here are shown: 1. the Robert Carter Kitchen; 2. the John Blair Kitchen; 3. the Ludwell-Paradise Kitchen; 4. the Taliaferro-Cole Kitchen; 5. the Bryan Kitchen.

3

4

2

5

View of roofs of the Archibald Blair outbuildings at right.

Below left, Wythe House outbuildings. The Ludwell-Paradise coach house is shown *below right.*

Above, fences and yards near the Printing Office.

Opposite page, Robertson's Windmill.

Fences were a concern of the inhabitants of Williamsburg almost immediately following the laying out of the streets and town by Francis Nicholson, lieutenant governor of Virginia. In 1705 persons building on the Duke of Gloucester Street were required to "inclose the said lots . . . with a wall, pails, or post and rails, within six months after the building . . . shall be finished." The enclosure by fences was intended to keep freely grazing animals from destroying the gardens.

The palisade or picket fence, in the middle distance *above,* was (and is again) the most common around Williamsburg homes and garden plots. The rough post-and-rail variety like that around the windmill, *opposite,* was by no means uncommon. The snake fence, native to this colony and associated with the day when timber was abundant, may have enclosed some neighboring fields but probably not many town lots, being entirely too wasteful of land.

1

2

CRAFTS AND CRAFTSMEN

In Williamsburg during colonial days there were skilled craftsmen in many trades. Sixteen cabinet-makers and upholsterers were engaged from time to time in the making and repair of furniture. Coachmakers, gold and silver-smiths, gunsmiths, mantua makers, hairdressers, carpenters, joiners, masons, blacksmiths, and farriers, all appear in York County records as having followed their trades in the town or locality. Extracts from the *Virginia Gazette* give an overall picture of local arts and crafts. November 28, 1745: "*Richard Caulton,* Upholster, from *London,* gives this public Notice to all Gentlemen, Ladies, and others, That he doth all Sorts of Upholsterer's Work, after the newest Fashion. . . . at reasonable Rates. . . ." July 25, 1766: "*B. Bucktrout,* Cabinet Maker, from London, on the main street near the Capitol in *Williamsburg,* makes all sorts of cabinet work, either plain or ornamental in the neatest and newest fashions. . . ."

Photographs on this page show: 1. the music teacher; 2. spinning and weaving; 3. the cooper; and 4. the gunsmiths.

4

3

Anthony Hay's Cabinetmaking Shop. By 1756, when he bought the buildings that stood on this site, Hay was an established cabinetmaker. His activities were not limited solely to the practice of his trade, for he would also repair furniture and make coffins. In time an addition to the shop was built, spanning the creek on brick piers. The interior is shown at *right. Below* are the tools of cabinetmaker and joiner.

The Sign of the Rhinoceros.

The apothecary shop of Dr. McKenzie.

Boot and Shoemaker's Shop.

The bootmakers at work.

Shop of Elkanah Deane, coachmaker, an emigrant from Ireland, who advertised in 1767 the making of "ironwork of every kind relative to the coachmaking trade."

The special skills of wheelwright, blacksmith, harnessmaker, upholsterer, and gilder went into the final product of a carriagemaker like Deane.

3

4

1

5

6

THE COLLEGE OF WILLIAM AND MARY

The College of William and Mary, founded by royal charter in 1693, is, after Harvard, the oldest college in the country. It was an English college set down in the wilderness of America with an educational system patterned closely after those of England. Three chief purposes motivated its establishment, "the education of the white youth of Virginia, the training of ministers for the church and the conversion of the Indian heathen." The illustrations show: 1. The statue of Lord Botetourt, an ardent supporter of the college. Of this famous statue, which once stood in the portico of the Capitol and is now in the Earl Gregg Swem Library, the *Virginia Gazette* noted, " 'tis much admired by all the curious and artists." 2. The Wren Building, the oldest academic structure in British America, was begun in 1694 and burned three times between 1705 and 1862. 3. The Great Hall, the one-time refectory of the college. 4. The President's House, erected in 1732. 5 and 6. Two views of the arcaded porch at the rear of the Wren Building, originally intended to face a courtyard.

When the restoration of Colonial Williamsburg began, the business life of the town extended along the entire Duke of Gloucester Street. Plans for the restoration included the provision of a special area to accommodate business activity. Hence, architects placed the shops, stores, offices, and service businesses at the end of the main street near the College of William and Mary. In this location the buildings served the townspeople, the college students, and the visitors conveniently but intruded little upon the ultimate restoration of the town.

Above, shops and offices are grouped in a business district just west of the Historic Area. Buildings are designed in the style of Virginia Tidewater architecture.

The area chosen, consisting of slightly more than two blocks divided by the street, was treated in a compatible manner. The shop groups were designed to harmonize with the architecture of the eighteenth and early nineteenth centuries, sufficient variety being introduced by the use of different building materials and paint colors so that the series of small or medium-sized buildings would possess individual character. In the rear of the shops, and screened by them, are parking areas. Passages give access to this parking and also provide more shop windows and additional exposure for stores.

The permanent closure to automobile traffic of the first two blocks of Duke of Gloucester Street made possible the replacement of curbs by swale gutters, the elimination of traffic signs, and a more complementary conjunction of the street with the rest of the historic way. Flowering trees, greens, and benches provide a quiet, unhurried space where civic functions, parades, and shoppers can mingle in an attractive environment.

THE INFORMATION CENTER

Key building among Colonial Williamsburg's visitor facilities, the Information Center is located on a forty-acre tract outside the Historic Area. The special space requirements of twin theatres and extensive exhibition areas called for a building in free architectural style to accommodate the size and relationship of these spaces. Visitors are invited to leave their automobiles at the Information Center and begin their tour of Williamsburg by boarding special buses at the lower level of the building.

Within the Information Center a continuous program of films, lectures, and exhibits orients the visitor to Williamsburg and suggests to him a variety of experiences that can deepen the meaning of his visit to the restored capital of Virginia.

ABBY ALDRICH ROCKEFELLER
FOLK ART COLLECTION

In addition to the eighteenth-century restored area, the Abby Aldrich Rock-efeller Folk Art Collection is a major point of interest for visitors to Williamsburg. Located on the grounds of the Williamsburg Inn, this separate museum houses one of the finest collections of folk art in America. The handsome brick building is designed in the style of the early nineteenth century, with Flemish-bond brickwork, stone trim and quoins, wood modillion cornice, and semi-circular stone arched doorway.

An oval garden enclosed by a serpentine wall provides an attractive approach to the building. A stone terrace is adjacent to the main entrance, which is decorated by wrought-iron gates. The interior architecture provides a harmonious background for the collection.

CREDITS FOR ILLUSTRATIONS

The photographs in the book, in large part made expressly for it, are with a few exceptions the work of four cameramen, Herbert Matter, Thomas Williams, Richard Garrison, and John Crane. Mr. Matter took his shots in mid-winter and as the buds began to open in the springtime. Mr. Williams was tireless in his efforts to furnish for the book photographs necessary to the illustration of the text or depicting unusual aspects of the Williamsburg scene. Mr. Garrison's and Mr. Crane's pictures were taken from time to time during the last few years. Additional photographs of unusual merit are the work of Jim Amos, Herb Barnes, Frank Davis, N. Jane Iseley, Charles Kagey, Robert C. Lautman, Taylor Lewis, Nivison, Steve Toth, and Delmore Wenzel.

The following abbreviations have been used in identifying the photographs and drawings listed in the credit index below: M—Herbert Matter; W—Thomas Williams; G—Richard Garrison; C—John Crane; JA—Jim Amos; CK—Charles Kagey; FD —Frank Davis; HB—Herb Barnes; NJI—N. Jane Iseley; RL— Robert C. Lautman; TL—Taylor Lewis; N—Nivison; T—Steve Toth; DW—Delmore Wenzel; CW—Colonial Williamsburg Files; L—Left; R—Right. Illustrations not otherwise identified are by the authors.

Front end paper, keys—W; door detail—M; **frontispiece**— CK; **v**—W; **vi**—W; **3**—FD; **4,** above—Paul Lacroix, *The Eighteenth Century, Its Institutions, Customs, and Costumes: France 1700- 1789;* **5**—T; **7**—T; **8**—W; **9,** L—W; **12**—W; **13**—CW; **15**—C; **16**—drawings by Thomas Mott Shaw; photograph—W; **17**—T; **18,** L—N; R—Historic American Buildings Survey; **19**—M; **20** —W; **21**—W; **22**—C; **23**—W; **24**—T; **25**—CW; **26,** No. 1—T; No. 2—Diderot, *Encyclopedia;* No. 3—W; No. 4—FD; No. 5—FD; wallpaper—T; damask—courtesy, Curator; **27**—M; **28,** No. 1—

T; No. 2—M; No. 3—W; **29**—CW; **30**—T; **31**—T; **32**—W; **33,** flask—CW; jar—HB; R—FD; **34**—CW; **35**—W; **37**—FD; **39**— W; **41**—TL; **42**—T; **44**—courtesy, the Century Company; **45**— courtesy, Massachusetts Historical Society; **46,** Palace—W; Palace drawing—courtesy, Bodleian Library; Raleigh Interior— CW; Raleigh interior drawing—Benson J. Lossing, *The Pictorial Field-book of the Revolution;* Prentis Store, L—FD; R—CW; **47,** John Crump House, L—CW; R—W; Greenhow-Repiton House, L—water color, artist unknown; R—C; Scrivener House, L—CW; R—C; **48,** Frenchman's Map—courtesy, College of William and Mary; **49**—courtesy, Bodleian Library; **50,** Plan—Architect's Office, CW; photographs—CW; **51**—M; **52,** above—T; other photographs—W; **53,** above—C; below—M; **54**—authors; **55,** above—C; below—M; **56,** above—C; below— FD; **57**—W; **58,** above—T; below—M; **59,** above—courtesy, Curator; below—T; **60**—W; **61,** above—T; below—CK; **62,** above—W; below—authors; **63,** above—W; below, L—Cook, Collection; R—CW; **64**—TL; **65,** above—M; below—C; **66**—T; **67,** above—W; below—T; **68,** above—M; below—W; **69**—M; **70,** above—M; below—W; **71**—M; **72**—W; **73**—T; **74,** above— T; below, L—C; R—W; **75,** above—M; below, L—W; R—NJI; **76,** above—G; below—T; **77**—T; **78,** above—M; below—CW; **79**—T; **80,** above—W; below, L—authors, R—FD; **81,** L—W; R —G; **82,** above—G; below—C; **83,** above—T; below—W; **84,** above, R—G; other photographs—W; **85,** above—M; below— W; **86**—T; **87**—CW; **88,** No. 1—FD; No. 2—FD; No. 3—T; No. 4—FD; **89,** above—T; below—W; **90,** above, L—C; R—T; below, L—W; R—FD; **91,** above—FD; below, L—M; R—JA; **92,** No. 1—M; No. 2—CW; Nos. 3 and 4—W; **93,** above—M; below —W; **94**—NJI; **95**—NJI; **96**—CW; **97,** above—T; middle—DW; below—RL.

BIBLIOGRAPHICAL NOTES

Colonial Williamsburg: Its Buildings and Gardens is based upon early historical works on Virginia, together with researches in the field of American architecture over a period of years. Sources of information and recommended authorities for extended reading are listed in the following notes. Footnotes to quotations in the text have been omitted for ease in reading. Few attempts have been previously made to assemble a listing of the scattered literature on the preservation and restoration of old buildings. The titles on this subject collected here will assist, it is believed, in the formulation of an improved and uniform restoration practice, with benefits from the extensive experience of other countries.

HISTORICAL BACKGROUND

Early writers on Virginia make scant mention of architecture, but they do supply a detailed picture of the historical background and life in the colony. Among the works of that time may be cited Robert Beverley, *The History and Present State of Virginia* (London, 1705; Chapel Hill, 1948); Hugh Jones, *The Present State of Virginia* (London, 1724; Chapel Hill, 1956); and *Journal & Letters of Philip Vickers Fithian, 1773–1774: A Plantation Tutor of the Old Dominion*, Hunter D. Farish, ed. (Williamsburg, 1957). A secondary work by Philip Alexander Bruce, *The Economic History of Virginia in the Seventeenth Century* (2 vols., N.Y., 1895) is most helpful on the economic life of the opening years of Virginia colonization. T. J. Wertenbaker, *The Old South; The Founding of American Civilization* (N.Y., 1942), gives an interesting and humanized account of Virginia history including extensive references to its early architecture and crafts. Some of the statements of Lyon Gardiner Tyler, *Williamsburg, the Old Colonial Capital* (Richmond, 1907), have since required revision, but the book should be read for the picture it gives of pre-restoration Williamsburg. Indispensable is Rutherfoord Goodwin's *A Brief & True Report Concerning Williamsburg in Virginia* (Williamsburg, 1941). The author has gathered together most of the pertinent documentary references to the town. The book summarizes facts related to the town's restoration and offers its own account of Williamsburg history.

Topics on Virginia history, personalities, trades, and materials can be traced to Virginia magazines and legislative sources with the aid of Earl G. Swem's invaluable *Virginia Historical Index* (2 vols., Roanoke, 1934–36). The rich store of material concerning eighteenth-century Williamsburg and Virginia contained in the *Virginia Gazette* has now been made conveniently available by the Institute of Early American History and Culture, which has prepared a detailed index for the years 1736–80. The files of the Departments of Research and of Architecture of Colonial Williamsburg offer compiled information on house histories, materials, building practices, and personalities of eighteenth-century tidewater Virginia.

ARCHITECTURE

Williamsburg architecture and gardens must be studied in relation to the region, also as a part of a development in America. R. A. Lancaster, *Historic Virginia Homes and Churches* (Philadelphia, 1915), is one of the better works for illustrations of notable plantation houses and gardens. Fiske Kimball, *Domestic Architecture of the American Colonies and of the Early Republic* (N.Y., 1927), is the most reliable guide for general study of early American architecture. *The Mansions of Virginia* by Thomas T. Waterman (Chapel Hill, 1945) is a well-illustrated work that discusses the Palace and many of the lesser dwellings of Williamsburg. A series of Williamsburg Architectural Studies was inaugurated in 1958 with Marcus Whiffen, *The Public Buildings of Williamsburg* (Williamsburg, 1958). This comprehensive presentation of Williamsburg's public buildings was followed by a companion volume by the same author, *The Eighteenth-Century Houses of Williamsburg* (Williamsburg, 1960). The latter study includes detailed descriptions of the original houses in the town. The first illustrated discussion of the restoration of colonial Williamsburg appeared in the *Architectural Record* of December 1935 (vol. 78, pp. 356–458) and of October 1937 (vol. 82, pp. 66–77). Illustrations in the *Record* are by the photographer F. S. Lincoln. Samuel Chamberlain's *Behold Williamsburg: A Pictorial Tour of Virginia's Colonial Capital* (N.Y. 1947) is comprehensive and has informative captions. In *Tidewater Towns* (Williamsburg, 1972) John W. Reps discusses fully and admirably the systematic planning of towns in colonial Virginia and Maryland—with special attention to Annapolis and Williamsburg.

GARDENS

In *Brothers of the Spade* (Barre, Mass., 1957), E. G. Swem has edited the horticultural correspondence from 1734 to

1746 between Peter Collinson in England and John Custis at Williamsburg. Joan Parry Dutton has written of the uses of flowering plants in *The Flower World of Williamsburg* (Williamsburg, 1973). The archaeological evidence for cultivation has been described by Audrey Noël Hume in *Archaeology and the Colonial Gardener* (Williamsburg, 1974). Joseph and Nesta Ewan have documented plant collecting in *John Banister and His Natural History of Virginia: 1678–1692* (Urbana, 1970). See also, "Joseph Prentis's Garden Book," a typescript copy in the Colonial Williamsburg Department of Research, and S.W. Fletcher, *A History of Fruit Growing in Virginia* (Staunton, 1932). Two botanical biographies, both by Edmund and Dorothy Smith Berkeley, *John Clayton: Pioneer of American Botany* (Chapel Hill, 1963) and *Dr. John Mitchell: The Man Who Made the Map of North America* (Chapel Hill, 1974) supplement our knowledge of later plant collectors. *Mark Catesby: The Colonial Audubon* (Urbana, 1961) by George F. Frick and Raymond P. Stearns strengthens the historical record with the story of Catesby's natural history drawings. E. M. Betts, *Thomas Jefferson's Garden Book* (Philadelphia, 1944) and Edith T. Sale, ed., *Historic Gardens of Virginia* (Richmond, 1923) combine with *Gardens of Colony and State*, edited by Alice G. B. Lockwood (New York, 1931–1934) and U. P. Hedrick, *A History of Horticulture in America to 1860* (New York, 1950) to describe the broader view of early gardening.

The Historic American Buildings Survey (in the charge of the Library of Congress) has undertaken the creation of a permanent graphic record of the existing remains of early dwellings in America. This has become a notable and extensive source of photographic illustration of early buildings, as well as of measured drawings of many examples.

RESTORATION OF OLD BUILDINGS

There now are many new works published that deal with restoration and preservation; too many, in fact, for all to be mentioned here. The National Trust for Historic Preservation, Washington, D.C., should be consulted for guidance on questions pertaining to methods of building preservation or restoration. *Historic Preservation Today* (Williamsburg, 1966) contains a number of thoughtful and informative papers and comments on them delivered at an international seminar on historic preservation held in Williamsburg in 1963. *Preservation and Conservation: Principles and Practices, 1972* (Washington, 1975) reflects further study and developments in the field. *The Restoration Manual* by Orin M. Bullock (Norwalk, Conn., 1966) is an excellent illustrated guide to the principles and practices that should govern the restora-

tion and preservation of historic buildings. *A Technical Handbook for Historic Preservation*, by Lee H. Nelson, published in series by the Government Printing Office, Washington, is a comprehensive guide to preservation and restoration techniques.

Other preservation-oriented publications include *The Necessary Monument: Its Future in the Civilized City*, by Theo Crosby (Greenwich, Conn., 1970); *Urban Renewal and the Future of the American City*, by C.A. Doxiadis, (Chicago, Ill., 1966); *Presence of the Past* by Charles Hosmer, (New York, 1966). *A Guide to Federal Programs* by the National Trust for Historic Preservation (Washington, 1974) provides a list of programs and activities related to historic preservation.

PRESERVATION OF OUR ARCHITECTURAL HERITAGE

Since the end of the last century the doctrine of preservation has been gradually replacing that of restoration alone. The principle, which has become a sort of international code, is that historic buildings require and deserve preservation and care.

Historic buildings in Williamsburg which have been preserved are important for two, sometimes overlapping, reasons. The first is their design and fitness of purpose. The other is their association with past life and history. This second quality varies and has been acquired slowly. Because of this association each building has been a source of new interest and delight to viewers. In this way a "patina" has been built up. This romantic quality has little to do with the rules of proportion and architecture, but it does evoke the past: the people and the way they lived, dressed, and conducted themselves.

It has been held important here at Williamsburg that we keep in mind this dual nature of the old buildings. Forgetting this in the restoration, we might destroy the patina of association and its indigenous significance and leave only the building's renovated shell. To touch an old building at all without destroying its charm and authenticity is exceedingly difficult. Three centuries ago John Dryden in *Absalom and Achitophel* penned these lines of caution:

> *If ancient Fabricks nod, and threat to fall,*
> *To Patch the Flaws, and Buttress up the Wall,*
> *Thus far 'tis Duty; but here fix the Mark:*
> *For all beyond it is to touch our Ark.*
> *To change Foundations, cast the Frame anew,*
> *Is work for Rebels who base Ends pursue.*

INDEX